Kickstart Your Time
Management

Other titles currently available in the *Kickstart* series:

Kickstart Your Career by Jeff Grout and Sarah Perrin
0–47084–301–2

Kickstart Your Money by Rachel Fixsen
0–47084–366–7

Kickstart Your Motivation by Sue Stockdale
0–47084–384–5

Kickstart Your Corporate Survival by Patrick Forsyth
1–84112–480-X

Kickstart Your Stress Management by Ann McCracken
1–84112–482–6

Kickstart Your Time Management

The Complete Guide to Great Work Habits

Frances Kay

CAPSTONE

First published 2003 by

Capstone Publishing Limited (a Wiley company)
8 Newtec Place
Magdalen Road
Oxford
OX4 1RE
United Kingdom
http://www.capstoneideas.com

Library of Congress Cataloging-in-Publication Data
Kay, Frances, 1949–
 Kickstart your time management / Frances Kay.
  p. cm. – (Kickstart series)
 Includes bibliographical references and index.
 ISBN 1-84112-481-8 (alk. paper)
 1. Time management I. Title. II. Series

 HD69.T54K39 2003
 650.1 – dc21   2003043562

British Library Cataloguing in Publication Data
A catalogue record for this book is available from the British Library

ISBN 1-84112-481-8

Typeset in New Caledonia by Florence Production Ltd, Stoodleigh, Devon.
Printed and bound by Biddles Ltd, Guildford and King's Lynn.

Contents

About the Author

Frances Kay is a professional organizer/administrator with over 35 years' work experience in a variety of professions, including the diplomatic service, politics and law. Despite working full time since the age of 17, Frances has found time to raise four children, travel regularly and move house eleven times. In her own words, she must be doing something right to manage to do all this and write a book!

She founded her own business solutions consultancy, Kayac Limited, in 1996. The company managed projects for busy professionals in areas of research, business development, human resources and event organization. Kayac was rebranded in 2002 to become Acumen2 – the rapport business. Acumen2 researches and sources customized professional introductions, corporate connections and strategic alliances for its clients – the essence of profitable business relationship building.

Frances lives in Gloucestershire with her husband and two children. She divides her time between the country and London. Besides running Acumen2, she writes business books, and gives presentations and talks on how to be better organized and on women's issues (including the changing face of the workplace).

acumentoo@aol.com

Acknowledgements

My sincere thanks to the wonderful friends, colleagues, clients, associates and experts in many other fields who contributed to the research for this book and whose knowledge was invaluable, particularly:

Lesley Barratt, Mike Bennett, Jo Biddolph, Kim Birchall, Kim Britton, Jocelyn Bury, Sophie Chalmers, Andrew Comer, Helen Elias, Nicola Goold, Les Green, Helen Guinness, Patrick Healey, Laurel Herman, Judith Hubbard-Jones, Jane James, Neilson Kite, David Kirk, Deborah Loth, David Lowe, Rowena Lusty, David Mattock, Dede Millar, Laura Pank, Annabelle Payne, Bridget Postlethwaite, Andrew Redman, Gwen Rhys, Lily Segerman-Peck, Sara Shailer, Mike Sitton, Nicola Stevens, Mary Welland, Matthew Wheelock, Linda Whitney, Greg Yager and lastly, but not least, Mark Kay, for his help and patience.

Introduction

Tomorrow is always the busiest day of the week.

Jonathan Lazair

Whoever you are, whatever you do, you no doubt have things that you want to achieve. To do this, it helps to be organized. Put simply, those who are best prepared are more likely to succeed than those who are not. Without an ability to manage time you can lurch from problem to crisis, and end the day having made little progress. This is disheartening because for much of the time you are reacting to situations that may be beyond your control.

Why let things get difficult when, with a little planning and focus, you can make good progress in achieving your goals? In essence, time management means being better equipped to handle the elements of surprise that can erode anyone's day. This book is for everyone who wants to produce more, enhance your performance and improve your output and efficiency.

You may think that you don't have time to read such a book, but it is a user-friendly volume! Read it from start to finish or dip into it at appropriate places. Don't waste another minute of your precious time – follow the tips suggested here and Kickstart your Time Management today.

Chapter 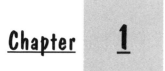 **1**

Time Management: What Is It?

I was going to write you a short letter, but I didn't have time so I wrote you a long one instead.

Mark Twain

I asked a friend of mine, a talented graphic designer who works in a thriving local design practice, to give me his definition of time management. He raised his hands to his face in horror. 'Oh no, don't ask me,' he pleaded. 'First, I'm terrible at time management. This isn't because I don't think it's important, or even that I don't know how to do it. The problem is that my brain just isn't wired up to think of time as being the slightest bit important.'

This intrigued me because I thought that everyone had an awareness of time. He continued, 'Ask any of my colleagues. I rarely know what time it is without looking at my watch. Hours seem to pass like milliseconds. Any task always takes much longer than I expect, or rather than I hope. In addition, I am a professional procrastinator of Olympic standards.'

I pressed him to elaborate. 'Well,' he replied hesitantly, 'when I finally manage to get involved in a task that is long overdue, because I am so stressed out that I haven't tackled it, I find my attention instantly being drawn to the nearest magazine, website, piece of irrelevant paper etc. The result can be . . . er . . . not a lot.'

He went on to explain that he consoled himself with the thought that all this was a sign of a massively creative mind, and that deep down in his subconscious he is putting new things together and worrying about dizzyingly important questions of the universe or the next entrepreneurial opportunity. In fact he fears that it's really a tendency to bunk off.

Fascinated by his candour and honesty about his time management failings, I spoke to another friend of mine, a high-powered professional, who works in London for a firm of property developers, running their marketing department. Because she has a young child, she sometimes works from home but regularly battles to meet deadlines and juggle priorities both in the office and at home.

I asked for her opinion on time management. 'Look,' she said, 'you shouldn't be asking me. Only last year my company sent me on an extremely expensive time management course that they could see I really needed. Unfortunately I arrived so late I wasn't even allowed in, so I missed it all!'

Does either of these examples strike a chord? I meet lots of people who are often short of time and are trying to get more things done in the day, but have no idea of what it takes to be organized.

If you have problems with time management, help is at hand. I have a passion for organization and have been paid to organize projects, people and events for most of my career. The advice contained here should help you to find ways of coping better with these issues.

The time and stress crisis

Stress (a definition)

A mismatch between perceived demands and perceived ability to cope.

To get the right balance you need to reappraise how you perceive and interact with your environment.

Are so many of us short of time because we simply don't understand the importance of controlling it? Why should you bother about managing time? Does managing your time really matter? Is it important? *Yes!*

Most of us have problems with time management because of our inability to plan. You need to plan your time and avoid both interruptions by people and the telephone. Procrastination is the single biggest cause of time management problems and is dealt with in more detail in Chapter 3. Crises can and do occur. Unless you have an effective time 'buffer zone' you will be unable to do anything better than fire-fight when having to deal with them. The ability to make decisions is the best way to combat time management problems. If you can develop the way to prioritize then you will be capable of solving the most difficult issues – and sometimes the seemingly impossible ones!

> ### Kickstart tip
>
> If you can remove the stress – your ability to cope with time will be infinitely greater. You should then be sufficiently relaxed to make the correct decisions when you need to make them.

Maybe I should mention here that I believe time management isn't really about time. It is all about tasks. It is about achieving, output, results. To be successful you need to develop skills and habits that, when used correctly, work positively on your behalf. These skills are not only necessary for doing a job successfully, they are also essential if you want to be seen as a competent, capable person.

To achieve anything today, it helps to be organized. In the office as well as at home, it is not good to be perceived as a headless chicken, led by events rather than being in control.

> ### Kickstart tip
>
> You may work hard, but sometimes you need to learn to work S M A R T
>
> S   specific – do you know what you want to achieve?
> M   measurable – do you have an idea how much use it will be?
> A   achievable – are you sure you are really able to tackle it?
> R   relevant – does it really matter?
> T   time based – how long is it going to take?

The techniques of time management are many and varied. Like most skills they cannot be learned by rote. You need to absorb and adapt the rules and apply them to your own individual circumstances – a tailored approach. Every constructive habit you can develop helps you kickstart your time management.

Kickstart tip

It's not the hours you put in, it's what you put into the hours.

We all know how true this really is. There's nothing worse than getting to the end of the day and feeling that you haven't achieved enough. For many people this is one of the most stressful things about life. Some of us struggle more than others, and have to work constantly to force ourselves to plan ahead and generally be aware of the fact that time is passing.

Why are we always so short of time?

Procrastination is opportunity's assassin.

Victor Kyam

If it's urgent – do it now! Don't procrastinate. Today's emergency could be tomorrow's disaster if it's left undone!

We all have too much to do. We have too many choices and many of us are unable to prioritize. This leads to a huge number of Olympic-standard procrastinators.

Kickstart tip

To learn how to prioritise, imagine that you have time to do only one task before leaving the country for an indefinite period. Which task would you choose?

The causes of procrastination are mainly tasks that are too big or too daunting. Or it could be due to a personal preference, dislike of a particular activity. Fear of failure is another cause. Also, lack of understanding of the perceived value or purpose of the task and the task being too boring. (See Chapter 3 for good habits to kill procrastination.)

Added to that, most people today expect instant gratification. Those who have studied animal behaviour will know that the inability to wait for something is a basic instinct of any lower species. Humans are not a lower species and therefore should not succumb! Yet how many times have you witnessed embarrassing outbursts from fully grown adults because of some insignificant hold-up in proceedings? There are frequent instances of road-rage, supermarket trolley rage, post office and bus queue rage. If there is a built-in buffer zone of time, there is less need for anger. People would probably be able to wait and show a little patience and tolerance when things take longer than expected.

Some common assumptions

> **Kickstart tip**
>
> The key element in effective time management is measuring the outcome, not the activity. Manage your time according to what will produce the best outcome.

Perfection is not necessarily the key

Time management does not mean being perfect and always getting everything done. It is more about being prepared for any eventuality. If, for instance, you know someone or have colleagues who panic because something unexpected happens, building extra time into the daily schedule (as a buffer) to counter-balance any time eroded unexpectedly would go some way to averting a time crisis.

It is often other people's inefficiency, rather than your own, or someone's arrogance or lack of respect for others that creates time management problems. One colleague told me how worried she was the other week because of a nearly missed deadline. Her boss had asked her to finish a piece of work by Friday provided that she was handed the task on Monday. Because of something beyond her control it wasn't ready for her until Tuesday. This caused her schedule to be one day short and through no fault of her own she spent two evenings working late at the office to complete the task. I indicated that there was a need here for assertiveness and boundary building.

When 'good enough' is sufficient

When working recently to produce a report for a specific dead-line, a trainee was called by a director of his company to an urgent meeting. It turned out that this meeting should have, and could have, been scheduled in advance. Even more annoying, it transpired that it wasn't really urgent or important and could easily have waited. As a result the trainee was faced with a dilemma: he didn't have enough time to do the work. If he decided to complete the task to his own high standards he would miss the deadline, or he could hand in a 'good enough' job by the time agreed.

To avoid getting stressed or wasting any more time he spoke to his boss. He explained that the unexpected meeting had upset his schedule and advised that the work would not be ready by the agreed deadline. He knew how important it was that the work was received on time because it was required for a meeting with other people that could not be rescheduled. He offered his boss the work that he had already completed in the hope that it was a 'good enough' job. His boss accepted and he delivered his report.

This proves the Pareto principle (otherwise known as the 80/20 rule): the manager was prepared to accept 80 per cent of the work. It was sufficient to get him through the meeting with his associates. The extra 20 per cent (had the trainee insisted on completing it) would not have added any significant amount to the end result.

Learn to know when 'good enough' is all that is needed. Stop fiddling endlessly with something if it already meets others' requirements and use the time that would otherwise have been spent on tinkering for something more important.

The Pareto principle (Figure 1.1), known as the 80/20 rule, was invented by Vilfredo Pareto (1848 –1923), an Italian economist. It is that 80 per cent of wealth is owned by 20 per cent of the population.

Kickstart tip: Using this principle

80 per cent of business comes from 20 per cent of clients
80 per cent of accidents are caused by 20 per cent of drivers
80 per cent of all beer is consumed by 20 per cent of the population
80 per cent of results come from 20 per cent of time
20 per cent of your day is spent on important tasks
80 per cent of our day just gets used up!

Main issues

The cost of poor time management is easily quantifiable in terms of wages or salary. However, these costs are probably the least of the problem. For most people, particularly during working hours, other costs can include:

- loss of control
- stress

- underachievement
- waste of resources
- opportunities lost
- poor communication
- lack of motivation
- missing out on quality time at home
- low morale
- slow response to change

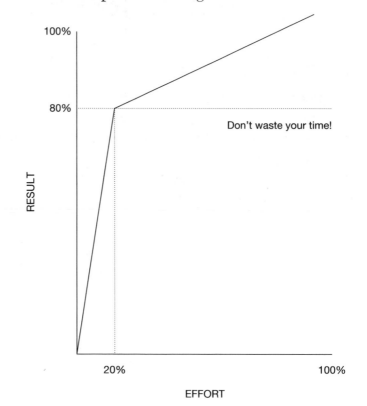

Figure 1.1   The Pareto principle (or the 80/20 rule)

The list is endless. If you don't manage your time (i.e. take control of what you *do* with your time) you will be inefficient. Tasks will take longer than necessary, mistakes will occur, and things will get left out or lost.

Managing time creates opportunities for you to do the things you really should be doing. Remember, it's not only about time, it's about tasks. By improving your performance you should be able to plan and manage your time better and achieve the outcome you want.

Kickstart tip

'If you do what you have always done, you will get what you have always got. If you don't like what you are getting, then you must change what you are doing.' (Borrowed from the principles of neuro-linguistic programming)

In the following chapters you will learn about yourself, how to plan, prioritize and write task lists. You will start by forming good habits, creating systems that work smoothly and discovering strategies for coping with unexpected situations.

Summary

- Time management isn't just about time – it's about tasks.
- It is a real asset to anyone's productivity and effectiveness.
- Time management is about staying in control.
- Time management helps you cope with interruptions, problems and crises.

- Time management avoids procrastination.
- Eliminates fire-fighting.
- Time management helps you learn to say 'no' and create boundaries
- Sometimes 'good enough' is all that is needed (Pareto).
- Learning new habits and skills will enable you to achieve more.
- If you can remove the stress, your ability to cope with time will be infinitely greater.

Chapter 2

What Sort of Person Are You?

What the caterpillar calls death, we call a butterfly.

Who are you? Who do you want to be and what do you want your life to be all about? These questions apply not only to your life in general but also at work.

For example, when planning your day, do you choose the routine tasks first? Or do you try to get the difficult or unpleasant jobs out of the way early on?

Are you creative? Or do you prefer to 'go with the flow'?

Is it difficult to be focused on what is going on? Are you easily distracted by others or events? Do you get carried away and suddenly realize that it is too late to go to the shops, or that the trains have stopped running for the evening?

How about lists? Do you use a 'to do' list for each day? If so, what kind of jobs are left unfinished at the end of the day?

Are you aware of Parkinson's Law that 'Work expands to fill the time available'?

Do you know when your mind is most productive and do you plan to do the most exacting jobs at that time of the day?

These are some of the questions you need to answer before you can make a start on developing the necessary habits. Spend some time thinking about these and then do the Time Management Habits exercise in Figure 2.1 on the next page and find out your score.

1	I begin each day with a daily task list	Yes	No
2	I block out a chunk of time each day for dealing with tasks	Yes	No
3	Every quarter I review my goals/objectives	Yes	No
4	I rarely work late or at weekends	Yes	No
5	I delegate/subcontract tasks whenever possible	Yes	No
6	I find it difficult to get the desired outcome at meetings	Yes	No
7	My telephone habits are bad and waste time	Yes	No
8	I have difficulty in preventing interruptions from happening	Yes	No
9	I wish I could learn how to say no	Yes	No
10	I often feel like a hamster on a wheel	Yes	No

Scoring

Questions 1–5
Score 2 points for all questions that you answered with a no   _____

Questions 6–10
Score 2 points for all questions that you answered with a yes   _____

Total point score: _____

14 points and above: You need help with your time management
8–12 points: Not bad, but room for improvement
Below 8 points: You have good time management skills and your techniques should improve even further by following the suggestions in this book

Figure 2.1   Time management habits

Knowing yourself is the key to success

It is so important to know what sort of person you are. That way you can look for the best strategies to help you overcome your weak areas and start getting things done.

We are all different as individuals, but we fall into similar character types. Some people function effectively well into the evening yet cannot cope with a dawn start. There are others who are raring to go at dawn because they awake with a natural energy surge. What type of person are you? Have you ever worked out the peaks and troughs of your day?

For example, do you know anyone who fits the description of the *Late Tasker?* This type of person needs the buzz of a deadline to complete any task and does his or her best work when under pressure.

Does this scenario strike a chord with you, or do you have work colleagues to whom this applies? One manager I work with hates getting up in the morning and never arrives at his office early or before his staff. He deliberately allows his working day to be absorbed by constant interruptions, meetings, telephone calls etc. He says that he finds this relaxing in a way and it enables him to interact and communicate well with his staff.

He prides himself on the fact that all his staff get to know him and he likes to promote an informal working atmosphere. He does not approve of 'closed-door' policies and his offices are open plan. He knows that whatever amount of time he has available to complete a particular task, he will fritter away that time until he simply *has* to get something done. It is only when the telephones have stopped ringing, the staff are on their way home and the office is quiet that he can sit down and concentrate on the serious stuff of the day.

He admits that when he realizes he's got only a couple of hours to finish something his brain really functions well. He is driven by the deadline whatever it is and has to have a time limit otherwise he never gets down to anything.

Activity analysis exercise

When you have completed the answers to the activity analysis in Figure 2.2 on pages 21–23, you will have some idea of whether you're task related or people related.

Kickstart tip

You should always reserve your high-performance hours for your most difficult tasks.

You are probably familiar with the Belbin team roles, a concept that evolved from work by Meredith Belbin and his researchers at Henley Management College over a period of years. While studying the behaviour of managers from all over the world undergoing psychometric tests and managerial exercises, different types of behaviour patterns emerged. These clusters of behaviour were given names, which relate specifically to the essential core personality traits, intellectual styles and behaviours required for successful teams.

Tick the answer that best describes how you respond to the following situations:

1 I like to
   a work however late to finish a job
   b not worry about deadlines
   c work with someone/get help to finish
   d do what I want, but get the job done

2 I sometimes get upset when other people work more slowly than I would like
   a yes
   b no

3 I get work done best when working with others/as part of a team by
   a showing great patience
   b pushing others to their limit
   c letting others set the priorities
   d setting work goals together

4 I like to help others with their work
   a yes
   b no

5 When people come to see me (at home or in the workplace)
   a I like to chat with them
   b I let them sort out their own problems
   c I spend a lot of time listening to them
   d I become impatient

6 I constantly check to see how others are getting on with their work
   a yes
   b no

Figure 2.2   Activity analysis exercise

7   When someone delegates a task to me, I prefer to
   a   be given total responsibility
   b   set early deadlines
   c   plan to do the work with others
   d   be patient

8   I like others to be in charge
   a   yes
   b   no

9   I avoid wasting time by
   a   getting through things quickly
   b   showing concern for others
   c   leaving others alone
   d   rewarding others for their help/teamwork

10   I am always early for meetings
   a   yes
   b   no

11   I encourage my friends/co-workers by
   a   being friendly towards them
   b   setting hard-and-fast deadlines
   c   working as a team
   d   avoiding conflict

12   Friendship is more important than deadlines
   a   yes
   b   no

Figure 2.2   (*continued*)

13 When my work schedule gets behind due to others, I feel
   a   very stressed
   b   concern for others
   c   like it is someone else's fault
   d   that the problem needs solving together

14 I plan my tasks way ahead of the deadline
   a   yes
   b   no

15 I get added value in my work by
   a   developing a network with other people
   b   encouraging a relaxed atmosphere
   c   using a team approach
   d   stretching my team/co-workers

16 I always say thank-you when things are done on time
   a   yes
   b   no

Scoring

There are no right or wrong answers to these questions. What you score in this exercise simply reflects how you interact between people and tasks. Some people are more task oriented, others are more biased towards people and relationships.

Figure 2.2 *(continued)*

As defined by Belbin, there are three *action-oriented roles*, the Shaper, the Implementer and the Completer Finisher.

- The *Shaper* is dynamic and thrives on challenges and pressure.
- The *Implementer* is disciplined and reliable, capable of turning ideas into practice.
- The *Completer Finisher* is painstaking and conscientious, inclined to worry and finds delegating difficult – but delivers on time.

Then there are the *people-oriented roles*, Co-ordinator, Teamworker and Resource Investigator.

- The *Co-ordinator* is confident and authoritative, clarifies goals and takes decisions.
- The *Teamworker* is co-operative, diplomatic and avoids confrontation.
- The *Resource Investigator* is extrovert, communicates well and searches for opportunities and contacts.

Finally there are the *cerebral* roles, Plant, Monitor Evaluator and Specialist.

- The *Plant* is creative and imaginative, solves difficult problems but ignores incidentals and is poor at communicating.
- The *Monitor Evaluator* is strategic and discerning, sees all options but lacks the drive and ability to inspire others.
- The *Specialist* is single-minded and dedicated, provides rare skills but can contribute only on a narrow front.

Which of these types do you identify with? Which ones do you work with? Which personality types from each of the three groups do you consider would make good time managers and which would have poor time management skills?

There is one shining example here out of all the groups that should be evident. Completer Finishers are ideal time managers. They will take trouble with a task and carry it out to the nth degree. They are painstaking, conscientious and take pride in correcting any errors or omissions. Above all, they finish tasks on time!

Understanding the difficulties

There are two main influences that combine to keep you from completing your planned tasks – other people and events, and yourself. You may, for example, put things off because you:

- are unsure of what to do
- dislike the task
- prefer another task (despite the clear priority)
- fear the consequences

Fitting in the small tasks

Not long ago I was working on a project with a busy lawyer at a large legal practice. He impressed me with his ability to juggle many tasks at once. When I asked him how he managed so well, he told me that years ago he'd learned a valuable lesson from his father.

His father was a director of a large company who worked long hours. Somehow he was always able to spend 'quality time' with his son in the evenings, weekends and holidays. When Patrick asked his father to tell him how he could get a lot done too, his father went into the kitchen and picked up an empty jar. He asked Patrick to get his bag of glass marbles and bring it to him in the garden. Together they went and sat in the sand-pit.

First he asked Patrick to put some sand in the jar until it was half full. Then he asked him to see how many marbles he could put in the jar and still put the top on. Only a few of the marbles fitted in. His father then emptied the jar, and told Patrick to put the marbles in first and then the sand. The boy was fascinated to see that all the marbles fitted in the jar as well as the sand. He was easily able to fit the top on.

Patrick never forgot the lesson: always tackle the bigger jobs by scheduling time for them in the diary. Fit the smaller stuff around them. It really does work!

Set yourself a challenge

Once you have worked out what kind of time manager you are, you can look at what you might like to change.

Kickstart tip

Start with the end in mind

- What kind of person do you want to be?
- What do you want your life to be all about?
- What do you enjoy?
- What gives you satisfaction?
- What makes you happy?
- What do you want to achieve?
- What do you need to do or change to get there?
- What are the actual tasks required to do this?

Write all this down and keep it handy (in a diary or planning folder, something you will use all the time).

Get yourself a daily time sheet and decide how much of the day you are going to devote to each task you have to do. This applies equally to your weekly or monthly schedule. Block out times with the appropriate task and the amount of time required. Make sure that you log exactly how much time you do spend and see how accurate your predictions were.

Do you, for example, spend too long on tasks because you *like* them? Be honest – this can be a major cause of wasted time. We flatter ourselves that no one else can do something as well as we can. We prefer not to delegate it in case this proves not to be the case!

A different approach?

If you find yourself unexpectedly in a situation where there is a glut of work compounded by a tight deadline, it helps to be flexible. A change of tack may be all that is needed to bring about an effective improvement.

Try getting in to work an hour or so earlier in the morning, say for one week, (I take the point that this would be anathema to the non-morning people!) and tackle some of the work you need to get through. That way, you'll create about two or three extra hours' work time. You may be amazed at what you get done before 9 am when the day really kicks in.

Summary

- It is a big fallacy that a task gets easier if you leave it. Actually the reverse is true.
- Make use of your personal strengths – they are often ignored or undervalued.
- Be realistic – you can't do everything.
- If you have a big project, try something different. If it can be tackled without the office infrastructure, work from home.
- Create a buffer zone for yourself. It is surprising how much can be achieved in a relatively interruption-free area.

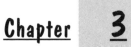

Chapter **3**

Making a Good Start: Good habits vs Bad

Procrastination is the art of keeping up with yesterday.
> Don Marquis, 1878–1937

Procrastination: a cautionary tale

You are probably all too familiar with the type of person who enthusiastically and with the best of intentions takes work home at 6 pm, but has still not completed it by midnight.

At 6 o'clock he approaches his desk and carefully organizes everything in preparation for the intensive work period to follow. Once everything is in its place, he next carefully adjusts each item again, giving him time to complete the first excuse; he recalls that in the morning he did not have quite enough time to read all items of interest in the newspaper. He also realizes that if he is going to get down to work it is best to have such small items completely out of the way first.

He therefore leaves his desk, browses through the newspaper and notices as he does so that there are more articles of interest than he had originally thought. As he leafs through the pages, he also spots the entertainment section. At this point it will seem like a good idea to plan for the evening's first break, perhaps an interesting half-hour programme between 8 and 8.30 pm. He finds the programme, which inevitably starts at about 7 pm. At this point he'll think, 'Well, I've had a difficult day and it's not too long before the programme starts. I need a rest anyway, and the relaxation will really help me to get down to the important work.' He returns to his desk at 7.45 pm because the beginning of the next programme was also a bit more interesting than he thought it would be.

At this stage he still hovers over his desk, tapping his papers reassuringly as he remembers that phone call to a friend, which, like the articles of interest in the newspaper, is best cleared out of the way before the serious work begins. The phone call, of course, is much more entertaining and longer than originally planned, but eventually the intrepid worker finds himself back at his desk at about 8.30 pm.

At this point in the proceedings he actually sits down at the desk, shuffles through the papers with a display of physical determination and starts to read (usually the top page) as he experiences the first pangs of hunger and thirst. This is disastrous, because he realizes that the longer he waits to satisfy the pangs the worse they will get, and the more interrupted his concentration will be. The obvious and only solution is a light snack. In its preparation this grows like the associative structure of a mind map, as more and more tasty items are linked to the central core of hunger. The snack becomes a feast.

Having removed this final obstacle, the worker revisits his desk with the certain knowledge that this time there is nothing that could possibly interfere with the dedication. He looks again at the first couple of sentences on the first page, but our determined worker realizes that his stomach is feeling decidedly heavy and a general drowsiness seems to have set in. Far better at this juncture to watch that other interesting half-hour programme at 10 pm, after which digestion will be mostly completed and the rest will have rendered him capable of tackling the task in hand. At midnight we find him asleep in front of the TV.

Even when he has been woken up by whoever comes into the room, he will think that things have not gone too badly. After all he had a good rest, a pleasant meal, watched some interesting and relaxing programmes, fulfilled his social commitments to his friends, digested the day's information, and got everything completely out of the way so that tomorrow at 6 pm . . ..

If you are honest I expect that you, like most people, are able to identify with parts of the story. Does it sound familiar? Don't we all have a tendency to do the little things first, so that by the time we settle down to the really important work, it's so late we're too tired to think'? I'm sure that everyone knows or is related to individuals who have similar habits.

As someone once said, 'Bad habits are like a comfortable bed: easy to get into, but hard to get out of.'

Jobs that you hate doing aren't always the ones that take the longest, but they can steal your time in other, sneaky ways. If a hated job is looming, there's always the temptation to find every distraction under the sun rather than crack on with it. Other jobs then end up taking longer than they should, because you are putting off facing the unpleasant task.

One of the most important steps to take when kickstarting your time management is to stop procrastinating. Work on your own ideas for improving your weak areas and start to develop your own personalized time management programme. You should be able to expand and improve this over the following chapters.

Here are a few suggestions that you could put into practice straight away.

Five new habits

Notebook
Use a big black book. Everything – all your lists, thoughts and rough notes – will be in one place – no more sticky notes!

Chunking
Block out space in your diary. Manage each day by blocking out time to allow you to focus on an important project at a point that is best for you. For example, if you are not a morning person try to plan midday or afternoons for difficult meetings, complex drafting and problem solving. (See Figure 3.1).

Delay reaction
Reflect rather than react. Avoid committing yourself to anything until you have all the information you need. Hasty decisions are often regretted and lead to unnecessary stress.

Delegate
Stop muddling through. Enlist the help of others when you are finding it difficult to complete certain tasks. Seek out particularly those whose skills complement your own.

Targets
Set achievable goals. Clearly defined objectives will help focus your mind and keep you motivated.

The Weekly Work Sheet	Week of		Monday	Tuesday	Wednesday	Thursday	Friday	Saturday	Sunday
Roles	Weekly Goals	Weekly Priorities				Today's Priorities			
			Buffer Day	Focus Day	Focus Day	Focus Day	Buffer Day	Buffer/Free Day	Free Day
Work Role #1			8	8	8	8	8	8	8
			8.30						
			9	9	9	9	9	9	9
Work Role #2			10	10	10	10	10	10	10
			11	11	11	11	11	11	11
Work Role #3			12	12	12	12	12	12	12
			1	1	1	1	1	1	1
Home Role #1			2	2	2	2	2	2	2
			3	3	3	3	3	3	3
Home Role #2			4	4	4	4	4	4	4
			5	5	5	5	5	5	5
Home Role #3			6	6	6	6	6	6	6
			7	7	7	7	7	7	7
You			8	8	8	8	8	8	8
			9	9	9	9	9	9	9

Figure 3.1   Weekly diary

If you can practise these five habits every day, they will become progressively easier. Aim to turn your resolutions into new habits that become part of your life.

First, make time to plan

One of the best things I learned years ago from a time management expert is how to start the day. The way you deal with the first hour you are awake dictates how you cope with a large part of the day. Everyone should strive to make that first hour as perfect as possible and for many people that means doing nothing at all. Just let your mind and thoughts wander.

Whether you are an 'early bird' or a 'sleepy night-owl', the way to maximize your enjoyment of the early morning is to avoid news, mail, emails or phone calls. There's plenty of time for these to encroach on your schedule later. When starting the day, the fewer unwanted demands the better.

If you are a thinker, focus on what you want to achieve and allow your mind to dwell on positive things. Develop a routine that suits you best. For some people, taking the dog for a quick walk or a run round the block is a great way to kickstart the day. For others doing some gentle exercise, deep breathing or yoga is helpful. Some people may appreciate a cup of tea and quiet thoughts, or take an envigorating shower. Whatever it is, creating your own personal routine is a way of mentally preparing yourself for the day. Make this a habit and repeat it every day (if possible) until it becomes a practised routine.

Kickstart tip

In creating your own perfect space, you learn to develop a buffer zone and as a consequence are equipped with a reserve of valuable time.

My favourite morning activity (being an early riser) is to get up and put on wellies or trainers (depending on the weather) and take the dog for an hour or half an hour's run. As I live in the country I only meet the odd uninterested cow, so appearances don't matter. It gives me a chance to think and blow away the cobwebs.

More suggestions

To do list
Create a to do list that goes one step further. Either before going to bed or when getting up in the morning, put down on paper what you want to achieve that day. Categorize the tasks by grading them A, B or C. As are absolute musts. Bs are chores that are less urgent but still important. Cs are those tasks that, should time allow, would be nice to get out of the way.

Bundling
Try to bundle certain chores together. For instance, earmark an hour a day for making all your phone calls. Plan to do errands on your way home from the office Batch the

emailing together in one go. Avoid jumping from one task to another. This way you'll be able to maximize your time, depending on how you've prioritized your day.

Include relaxation or activity breaks

Allow some 'down time' during your day. Stare out of the window if you like, day-dreaming, or do whatever you need to recharge your batteries. Even with just two 15-minute breaks, you will return to your desk with renewed energy and work far more effectively.

Be a hermit

Plan when not to be 'on call'. If you're trying to work to peak capacity, switch on your voicemail and ignore all inter-ruptions. It's the only way people will ever learn that sometimes you're unavailable.

Action plan for time management

These are good, practical tips that are easy to use. They deal with important issues and they really do strike at the heart of the matter – making the most effective use of your time.

Out of the above tips, pick three or four that suit you best. Work them into your own schedule and practise them daily until they become habitual and automatic.

Each day, make sure you've planned to do at least three important things. Then work out the rest of the day so that these tasks actually get done. Achieving goals is one of the most satisfying things that can happen. Particularly while trying to effect habit changes, it's vital to *see* a difference.

If this book were about dieting, think how thrilled you'd be when the first few pounds began to drop off your weight. Look at time management in a similar way. Each task ticked off your list gets you closer to your goal. It may not be a target weight that can be measured on the scales, you are attempting something more complex – to trim off the excess waste of time. What you are aiming to achieve are sleeker days with hours to spare.

A remark attributed to Wallis Simpson, 'A woman can never be too rich or too thin', can perhaps be adapted to what we are discussing here – you can never have too much spare time. Work on gaining an extra hour a day. Think what you could do with an extra five hours a week.

What needs to be changed to succeed

So first you need to set goals that are sensible, achievable and worth the effort. If they don't fit these criteria, you're never going to find the time or bother to work at them. You need to be able to identify these goals for yourself. Maybe you could start by listing them into three categories, A, B or C: short-term, mid-term and long-term goals.

You need to work out how to get to your goal, have clear objectives on how you're going to do it, set yourself specific tasks and go for it. Don't hesitate – act now. Set a few goals of your own and see how you get on. If it doesn't work, or you feel you

Monday	Tuesday	Wednesday	Thursday	Friday	Saturday	Sunday
25	26	29	30	31	1 Easter Hols Start TC/Rus o/n	2 12.00 Rugby match 17.00 Cinema
3 09-16.30 BFH	4 10-11 BH 12-13 Jo @ GY 14-15 Karen @ Pospect 15-16 BH party	5 12-13 Lunch Amy & Regina 14-16 BH	6 13-14 John Rutherford 16-17 Nick & Netser	7 9-16-30 BH	8 20-22.30 Todd & Marian	9
10 11-12.30 John Winkworth Accountants	11 14-15.30 Dick Finch Lunch 19-20 Swots	12	13 8.30 To Paris	14	15 20.45 Return from Paris	16
17 11.30 PACE	18 9 start all day Sales and Marketing Conference	19 All day Sales and Marketing Conference	20 11.30 BH restaurants meeting	21	22	23
24	25	26	27	28	29	30
31	1	2	3	4	5	6

Figure 3.2 Monthly diary

aren't getting anywhere, sit down and reconsider. Find things that help you gain a few minutes a day. Go back to the analogy of the dieter: even in the first week, if you follow the guidelines and your own objectives, you should be able to see and feel a difference.

Kickstart tip

The difference between effectiveness and efficiency:

- Efficiency is doing things right.
- Effectiveness is doing the right things.

'Results come from doing the right things, not from doing things right' (Peter Drucker).

If you still feel that you're constantly 'fire-fighting', figure out what's really important. If you decide exactly how many tasks you need to get done, which ones are important and in which order you should do them, you will begin to feel more in control. You will work more effectively and will end up with the quality time you deserve.

You do need to be clear about your objectives. It is like driving a car – if you don't know where you're heading, you won't know how to get there.

Mark Forster, author of *Get Everything Done and Still Have Time to Play*, says 'We can't manage our time well unless we know what we want to achieve.'

Make a list

The best way to start, as established earlier, is to learn to prioritize. To do this you have to make lists to determine what is important. True planning is about identifying what is important, not about making a task list. Task management can sometimes become a substitute for planning. If we are so busy making our lists that we end up postponing decisions that need to be made or actions that need to be taken, then we are not planning, prioritizing or managing our time at all.

Kickstart tip

Try to make your daily To Do list the evening before, so that you see it first thing in the morning. Fire-fighting jobs and tiny things should not be included – keep them separate.

A friend of mine who is always busy says that her most important time management tool is her daily To Do list. She knows that she really can't function without it. She maintains one for her work and one for her home/social life. By writing down the night before all that she needs to get done the next day, she starts the day with a much clearer mind and a focused agenda. It is then not so easy to spend so much time on unimportant issues that can devour great chunks of time. To have the important tasks right there in front of you in black and white makes them much harder to avoid.

Another advantage of the list process is tracking time. If an item has been on your list for weeks and weeks, it begs the question of whether the task needs to be done at all. Maybe it should be crossed off, or perhaps it would take only a few minutes to deal with, or can be delegated, just to get it out of the way.

At work, and in life generally, the key thing is to focus on what are A list priorities vs the rest. Don't let yourself be waylaid by B list items. Identify what really matters, then look at how they can be achieved. If they are difficult spend some time on them each day – even if it's only half an hour or so. Think about them, take action on what can be done and little by little progress will be made – things will get done. Each day review the B list to see what non-core tasks need to be tackled to ensure that the A list happens. Review results at the end of each day and plan the next.

Kickstart tip

Make a list – but make it real. It doesn't have to be rigid to work.

Your task list has to be real. There is no point having things on it that need not be there. Remove all the 'wish list' ideas; they should be elsewhere. Remove anything that does not have a definable deadline. Decide on the number of items that should be scheduled for any one day. I say it should be 'real', but it does not have to be rigid. It needs to be flexible enough to allow for opportunities.

If your day is limited to what you can anticipate, all manner of unforeseen things might be excluded. There will always be unplanned calls or chance meetings. Some of these will be useful if they provide unexpected information or even perhaps new business. Sticking rigidly to your plan might mean that you miss something important. There is a need for structure, but not at the expense of opportunity.

After you've started to work on your plan, how will you know if you're hitting your time management goals? Quite simply – if you come to the end of your day with time to relax and most of the items on your list ticked off, your time planning is working. This means that you are controlling your time and not the other way round. Worth a try?

Og Mandino, whose successful books have inspired and motivated millions, says:

> *I will act now. I will act now. I will act now. Henceforth, I will repeat these words each hour, each day, every day, until the words become as much a habit as my breathing, and the action which follows becomes as instinctive as the blinking of my eyelids. With these words I can condition my mind to perform every action necessary for my success. I will act now. I will repeat these words again and again and again. I will walk where failures fear to walk. I will work when failures seek rest. I will act now for now is all I have. Tomorrow is the day reserved for the labour of the lazy. I am not lazy. Tomorrow is the day when failure will succeed. I am not a failure. I will act now. Success will not wait. If I delay, success will become wed to another and lost to me forever. This is the time. This is the place. I am the person.*

A friend of mine who is always busy forwarded me the above quote. It struck me as relevant for time management. On the one hand, Og does not appear to have more than one thing on at a time.

However, when he does, there is a clear priority to them. Alternatively he is being realistic and reminding us that time management is about action – action that may be doing, delegating or dumping.

Goals that are worth the effort

One good time management habit is to make plans for the whole month ahead. A month at a time gives you the ability to put tasks into better perspective. It allows you to plan each week with greater precision and detail. For example, you could start to allocate days for particular tasks, such as visiting clients or working on presentations (see Figure 3.3). Colour code them (with highlighters) if that is easier. You could use pink for urgent and important tasks, orange/yellow for important/non urgent, green/blue for non-working time (which may be equally important), family/social, leisure or thinking time.

If you have to spend days at a time working on projects away from your office, your daily task list will need to be adjusted accordingly. My weeks are split between London and the country. My schedule for Mondays and Fridays when I am usually at my desk in the country looks totally different to my mid-week schedules. I have approximately three days a week that I fill with meetings at my office or working with clients at their offices, giving presentations and attending networking events. These are my busiest days and are coloured pink/red. Mondays and Fridays are always busy too although I try to stay confined to my desk. The pace is fast, but at least I remain in one location. They are coloured yellow/orange, which reflects the fact that they are less stressful.

Saturdays and Sundays are blue/green, which indicates calm and peace! What this really means is that it is non-client time and not reliant on watching the clock. Whatever needs to be done can be accomplished equally well in the morning, afternoon or evening. I can exercise a degree of choice depending on how I feel, particularly if the tasks don't involve input from other people. This reduces the stress factor considerably. In addition, the majority of tasks on the schedule relate to non-fee-earning tasks.

Having said this, my weekend to do lists are fairly long and it's a great time to mop up a lot of smaller jobs that just don't merit time being spent on them during the week – my grains of sand, which surround the marbles in the task jar.

When making your daily list, try to stick to it. Be determined and refuse to agree to the demands or pleas of others. Do only those things that are on your list that day. If something unexpected does crop up, and it has to be done, add it to the list. That way (if it is a job that can be done fairly quickly and painlessly) you have the satisfaction of crossing it off. This satisfaction should never be underestimated! There is no need to beat yourself up about the jobs that didn't get done. Simply transfer them to the following day's list.

Kickstart tip

Concentration is vital. Always work on one thing at a time, preferably until it is finished. If that isn't possible, at least persevere until the task has progressed as far as possible.

Develop your own 'bring-forward' system or follow-up procedure for uncompleted tasks. This will be covered in more detail in Chapter 9.

If you can ensure that all resources are available before starting work it will make the task flow that much more easily (see Chapter 6). Remove potential distractions, whether they are your own thoughts, colleagues or associates trying to access your time, or outside influences.

The main cause of procrastination (which is where this chapter started) is that the job is either too big or too daunting. You may have a personal aversion to the task or dislike the activity. If you are afraid of failure you may try hard to avoid even starting. If you cannot appreciate the value or purpose of the task, this is very often a symptom of bad briefing from a superior or inappropriate delegation from a manager, (see Chapter 7). Or the task may simply be so boring that you never feel like tackling it. In that case think about it for a while. Perhaps it is a C list task that doesn't need to be done? If so, forget about it.

With really huge tasks, I begin by breaking them up into smaller pieces. This way it is sometimes easier to get started. It is possible, even if you really hate something, to do it for a short time. Try using a timer for ten minutes while you tackle that really nasty job. At least you will have broken through the aversion barrier.

When the job is both urgent and horrible – do it first! Getting it out of the way quickly means that it doesn't ruin the rest of your day. You can reward yourself by having a treat afterwards. Go for a coffee with a friend, make some pleasant telephone calls or check out your friendly emails.

Kickstart tip

If you can't face something, tell a colleague or a friend about it and your deadline for completion. Once you've gone public it will be harder to avoid doing the job.

For those who are avid list makers, sit down and write out your reasons for procrastinating vs your reasons for getting started. This is fine – but please make sure you do this only if there is time!

A good plan is to practise becoming adept at identifying leading tasks. What is the *first* thing that really has to be done? When you've completed it, go on to the *next first* thing and so on.

A final suggestion: if you simply can't face the work and you're panicking, sit down and do nothing at all. Do nothing except think about why you're not doing that task. If you've already carried out the 'balance sheet' exercise about reasons for procrastinating, enlarge on it by writing down your thoughts and feelings about the problem task facing you.

Summary

- Decide what is important to you.
- What do you want to achieve?
- By when do you want to achieve it?
- Make the most of your personal strengths.

- Plan regularly in blocks of time on a daily or weekly basis.
- Get a sheet of paper (or notebook) and make your list.
- Isolate the three most important tasks and complete them first.
- Enjoy the sense of achievement in marking a task as 'done'!

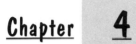

Chapter **4**

Stressed? Health-related Issues and Work/Life Balance

There cannot be a crisis next week. My schedule is already full.
Henry Kissinger, New York Times, 1 June 1969

Several months before I started writing this book, I remember having a conversation with a friend. At the time I was worried. Normally we speak regularly, maybe once a week. Even though I had left messages for her to ring me it was a few weeks before she returned my calls. When we finally spoke, she was apologetic.

It transpired that there was no particular cause, she was just overwhelmed by work. My friend felt she had lost her ability to cope. There was simply too much to do – she was working late in the evenings, bringing work home and going into the office at weekends. She was seriously overloaded. She described it as feeling that everything was closing in on her, stifling her. It didn't matter how hard she tried, she just couldn't get through the number of things she had to do. Her solution was to shut herself off and have no contact with her friends.

You may think that this is quite a common occurrence. Everyone feels like this at times, it's quite natural and a way of telling us to slow down or stop.

However tired or drained you feel, if you're exhausted, distracted or unable to cope matters are getting serious. If you become depressed, you are suffering an unacceptable level of stress. By reaching a point where you feel despondent and lose interest in your work, friends and family, you develop a sense of futility about life generally. Then it is time to sit up and take notice. Because stress, up to a point, can be a positive force, people sometimes have a tendency to forget when it is time for stress-busting action (Figure 4.1).

It is nothing to be ashamed of, but no one wants to reach this state of burnout. If you know that's where you're heading, don't panic! You're in good company. Many high achievers and busy professionals work over-long hours and are dedicated to their jobs. If you count yourself among them, you too have a tendency to push yourself to the limit.

Most people admit to suffering stress and over 70 per cent of readers of a women's magazine recently surveyed admitted that work was the main cause of their stress.

Effective stress management is an extension of time management. It is essential to learn how to react to certain stresses and discover your own safe level. One way to work out your personal tolerance level is to keep a diary.

Make a note of how you feel on a daily basis – happy, unhappy, unsettled, in control, out of control, anxious, frustrated, confident, successful?

Analyse the results. When did you feel happy and on top of things? What had you done that day? What factors had influenced you? How much time did you have to yourself? What did you eat or drink? What exercise did you take? Who did you spend time with?

Identifying the problem is vital. When you are stressed, you are on the way to losing your perspective and ability to focus. You are also running the risk of incurring health problems. You need to take action immediately to remedy this and to avoid getting caught in the ever-decreasing circle of working harder to achieve success. Working harder is not the solution – it simply won't help. Everything will take longer, you'll achieve less and your sense of stress and frustration levels will increase dramatically.

Defining positive and negative stress situations

I was recently discussing the subject of stress with an architect I work with and I asked him how he would define the difference between positive and negative stress.

- Recurrent headaches
- Ringing in the ears or frequent noises in the head
- Regular use of self-prescribed drugs
- Palpitations and chest pains
- Attacks of heartburn, stomach cramps, diarrhoea
- Feeling that you may pass out
- Getting any illness that is around
- Loss of former concentration
- Loss of former reliable memory
- Difficulty in thinking around problems
- Inability to reach satisfactory decisions
- A feeling of being very low or dulled
- A shut-down of all emotions except anger and irritation
- All laughter has dried up
- Active love and caring have lessened or disappeared
- Tears or rage appear frequently for very little reason

Figure 4.1   Stress symptoms that should not be ignored

'I had a situation at work the other week that showed me the difference,' he told me. 'There was a big report that had to be completed. It had been delegated to a couple of my junior colleagues, some time ago. It was probably my fault, I gave it to them far too early. When I asked them where the document was, they admitted it was unfinished. The peculiar thing about stress is that everyone reacts to it differently.'

He explained how he had asked them to get on with the work as a matter of priority. The finished report was needed the following day. One rose to the challenge and got on with his work like a demon, producing a clear and excellent piece of work. The other, meanwhile, felt stressed and anxious and it soon became evident that he wasn't going to complete his part of the job in time.

'Once I could see we were going to get nothing useful out of him, I diverted him to another job and drafted in a young trainee. I then worked alongside them both to pull the report together,' the architect said.

As well as getting the report finished on time, he commented, 'I learned several valuable lessons too. First, the three of us worked well as a team. Second, one obviously needs a deadline to work to. I understand the way he thinks and I'll be able to utilize him better within the company. Third, the trainee was so keen to impress us with her enthusiasm, that I've found out a lot more about a new member of staff than I would ever have done otherwise. I got the job done and I've gained knowledge about my staff that I didn't expect.'

'What else did you learn?' I asked.

'I've a good worker, who's loyal and has valuable skills. If he hates deadlines, then I'll make sure he has plenty of warning when I give him work and keep an eye on him to avoid that situation arising again. Having asked around the office, it seems his problem is that he spends too long on a task. I guess he's a perfectionist.'

Pressure at mild levels can have a positive effect. It can energize us and encourage us to perform at our best. When we reach our expected deadlines or targets or crack a difficult problem, we quite justifiably feel exhilarated and a sense of success. However, situations can quickly become negatively stressful when these pressures overpower us. We feel unable to cope and out of control.

Coping with stress

For decades, backache used to be the cause of most absenteeism from work. Stress now keeps up to a million people at home on an average day. Some 90 per cent of visits to GPs are put down to stress and in 1998 stress-related illnesses cost £10.2bn in lost productivity.

Sickness absence – both long and short term – can mask other concerns besides stress, such as poor work environment, bullying and other health issues.

Nevertheless, having admitted (either to yourself or to others) that you have a problem, you need to identify your symptoms and make an action plan. There are a number of ways to reduce stress levels. The most important is by learning to control your time – of course. That is why you are reading this book!

> ## Kickstart tip
>
> You can control stress in three ways: by applying common sense, by looking after your body and by controlling your mind.

Controlling stress by common sense

When you're overworked sit down and think for a few minutes. As suggested in the previous chapter, begin by asking yourself which are the two or three most important things to be done today. What if they weren't done at all? Could someone else do them?

One of the simplest strategies is to control what you can, and ignore what you can't. Be happy with what you have. Sometimes it is worth remembering how much worse things could be.

Remember the phrase 'Do your best and leave the rest'. You're human, after all. When mistakes do occur, you can always learn from them.

Controlling stress by looking after yourself

If you are working long hours at a desk, make a decision to get up and stretch regularly and take some deep breaths.

Taking frequent exercise helps control stress by the release of endorphins. Even a short walk inside or preferably outside the office is good. It improves your mood and helps unclutter your mind.

Eating sensibly and often is also beneficial. Whether stress is mental or physical, good exercise and eating habits protect the body from increased stress levels.

Get enough sleep. Lack of sleep clouds your judgement and deprives you of the ability to think clearly and make decisions.

Controlling stress by controlling your mind

Visualize something positive. If you close your eyes and visualize a relaxing, pleasant scene or event, it makes you feel happy.

If you are trying to make things happen, imagine success not failure. Think about how you will perform a specific task. Focus on positive rather than negative results.

To analyse your ideas and, to think more clearly, you must focus your thoughts. The habit of thinking about too many things at the same time is extremely tiring.

If you are worried about an interview or meeting a particular person, try picturing it in your mind in miniature. The effect this has is to reduce the fear factor to a minimum.

Whatever methods you use, try to enjoy yourself.

Kickstart tip

Have a laugh. Laughter is one of the best tension releases there is. Regular laughter can permanently lower the heart rate and blood pressure.

Take control

Research shows that the less control you have in your life, the more stress you feel. Certain jobs are high in psychological demand (mental challenge) and low in decision making (control). These are the most stressful, so if you work in intensive care nursing or air traffic control or are a doctor or a teacher, your stress levels are going to be far higher than those of people who are more in control of their destiny. If you want low stress, become an artist or work in a museum or a library!

What do you have to cope with in your working day? Is your role largely autonomous and proactive? Or does it rely on others delegating work to you that you have to complete in a certain time? This will affect the amount of stress you feel at work.

When pressure becomes intolerable, it can be incredibly difficult to see a way through it. The best way to cope is to stop, take a step back and face each task at a time.

Coping with stress is not easy. You may well become irritable with family members and short-tempered with colleagues. You probably feel tired all the time and burst into tears or fly into a rage for what seems like no apparent reason.

Harbouring feelings of anger, aggression, conflict or frustration without any particular excuse is a typical example. Occasional feelings of stress are not harmful, but beyond a certain limit it has a marked effect mentally as well as physically.

Learning how to react to situations that cause anxiety and stress is vital. Acting positively, assertively and constructively will enable you to stay in control and reduce the build-up of stress.

Kickstart tip

The secret of coping with stress is simply to relax. The body can't be stressed and relaxed at the same time.

Answer yes or no to the following situations. Where you have answered 'yes', score them between 0 and 10 points, depending on the stress rating you give the area.

1   Have you ever been landed with a huge piece of work just a
    week before going on holiday?   Yes   No
2   Is your company being forced to make redundancies?   Yes   No
3   Are you experiencing unreasonable or unsympathetic
    behaviour from colleagues/family/spouse?   Yes   No
4   Is your boss refusing to support your bid for promotion?   Yes   No
5   Do you regularly have to work evenings and weekends?   Yes   No
6   Are you made to feel awkward if you request time off for
    family reasons, e.g. elderly parents, spouse or children unwell? Yes   No
7   Have you had to miss out on significant family events in the
    last 12 months due to work overload? Birthdays, wedding
    anniversaries etc.?   Yes   No
8   In the last year have you had to cancel a restaurant trip,
    concert or holiday/weekend away due to pressure of work?   Yes   No
9   Do you regularly have sleepless nights because of work?   Yes   No
10 Are you less decisive or do you have an unreliable memory
    or loss of concentration   Yes   No

How many of these issues relate to you? How many stress points have you scored?

0–40   OK;   40–70   Be careful;   Over 70   !!!!!!!!!

Figure 4.2   Stress levels exercise

If you are feeling overloaded and can't take on any more, you must learn to say no. Prioritizing your tasks is important – delegate something if possible. Draw up an action plan and set realistic goals, as described in the previous chapter.

Suggestions for beating stress

- Take some time off. It doesn't matter if it's a weekend or just a day. Distancing yourself from the cause of the trouble is often a great help.
- Walk to work. People who walk regularly are not only fitter but have a larger number of brain cells!
- Think about your leisure time – how much of your working week is spent doing nothing? If the answer is less than a day, add another four hours to your time schedule.
- Move to France. The French have imposed a 35-hour week to stop people from working over-long hours. If that is impractical, merely pretend to be French and leave work early!
- At the other extreme, the Japanese have a word, 'karoshi', which means death from over-work. It really happens – so make sure you don't succumb!

Work/life balance

Making sure your life is balanced is easier said than done. Balance (like life) is never a perfect situation, nor is it permanent. Everyone has their own definition of balance and what is good for one person may well be the opposite for someone else. What is acceptable is what is appropriate for you.

If you are fortunate enough to be happy and fulfilled most of the time, then your balance is about right. If you don't harbour feelings that you are neglecting anything or anyone of importance, then you are probably within your own balanced framework.

Is work the dominant feature of your life? There are times when you simply must work long hours at the office or you have to stay away from home on business. During those times you have less time for yourself and your home. At other times the balance shifts the other way and you neglect your work due to sickness or serious problems at home.

If either situation is temporary, you can use common sense to compensate in other ways and get back to the normal balance quite quickly. Remember, there is no right or wrong balance to aim for. It is all relative. To get some idea of your current position, complete the balance test (Figure 4.3). By following this at regular intervals, you can use it as an indicator of whether things have improved or worsened.

Much research has been done recently among global companies to help employees maintain a better work/life balance. It is proving too costly for corporations to lose valued employees because of the damaging effects of 'presenteeism' and the long-hours culture. Often employees get stressed out and leave their

Score the following statements from 4 (highest, or most true for you) to 0 (lowest, or least true for you). There is no pass or fail mark for this test, but scores of below 40 indicate room for improvement. Retake the test periodically to see if your work/life balance has altered.

Work
1   I have fun doing my job
2   I keep up with new developments in my field
3   I find time each day for one key task
4   I am able to get done what I set out to do on a weekly basis
5   I am satisfied with the reward for my efforts and contribution
6   I have good relationships with my colleagues and clients
7   I generally feel in control of my work and do not feel anxious or stressed
8   I am able to get back on track if crises or problems surprise me

Self
1   I enjoy my hobby/I do something for fun at least once a week
2   I am able to express my feelings when I'm angry or upset
3   I am able to organize my time effectively
4   I can say no when necessary
5   I find time for myself to be quiet during the day
6   I can cope well with daily minor issues: traffic, phone, kids
7   I am in good physical health and take regular exercise
8   I sleep well and sufficiently for my needs

Home
1   I have a good network of friends and acquaintances outside work
2   I have at least one dependable friend/relative within 50 miles
3   I regularly attend a club or social activity

Figure 4.3   The balance test

4 I have sufficient income to meet my basic needs
5 I give and receive physical and emotional affection
6 I have two or more close friends in whom I can confide
7 I have regular quality time with my family
8 I have calm conversations about important life issues with friends and
relatives on frequent occasions

Figure 4.3   (*continued*)

jobs, when it would cost the employer less in the long run to show a more enlightened approach and institute flexible hours and methods of working.

Many organizations are actively striving to become more employee-friendly and are pursuing strategies to increase the flexibility of their working practices. For example, some companies now monitor the working hours of their employees. The process is designed to identify people who work over-long hours. If employees seem unable to adjust their workloads themselves, after a period of time they are offered counselling on how to work more effectively.

There is probably no need to give 100 per cent to most situations. Remember the 80/20 rule, the Pareto principle that we looked at in Chapter 2.

Practice positive thinking: try telling yourself that you enjoy doing your job. Remind yourself of the benefits of success. Promise yourself a treat once you've done a particular task.

You don't have to do things all at once. You need not finish a project, just do an hour on it then go away and do something more interesting. Once you've made a start it is a lot easier to get back to it later.

> ### Kickstart tip
>
> If you're feeling stressed, fix your mind on the job in hand. Try to imagine you're a fortified castle and distracting thoughts are unsuccessful invaders. Repel those trying to scale the walls and break down your defences.

Assertiveness

Being assertive is a way of bringing situations under control that could otherwise get out of hand and cause unacceptable levels of stress. Remember, being assertive is not the same as being aggressive. Nevertheless, it is the opposite of being passive.

Speak up for yourself. Be prepared to let people know where you stand. It may be that others have simply not appreciated the situation from your perspective.

Tell someone how you feel. If you don't tell your boss how you're feeling, how can he or she possibly know? It isn't that easy to be inside another person's head. Situations or people may not be as difficult as you imagine.

Say what you want. Informing people of your wishes, aims or desires completes the picture. There are two sides to every situation and disclosure is sometimes the only way to sort a situation out.

Separate fact from opinion. In order to bring about a solution or compromise, it is essential to have the relevant facts. Hearsay, gossip and personal views do not help the negotiating process and can be viewed by the other side as irrelevant.

Kickstart tip

Recognize that things can be different for other people. How often have you asked two people to describe the same incident and got different stories? Don't forget that your perception of a situation can be quite unlike someone else's.

Be direct. Avoid waffle. Most people are prepared to listen, but be concise and restrict yourself to relevant information.

Be prepared to negotiate. Most successful solutions come through effective compromise. If you're prepared to give something to ensure a win–win situation, you may well be agreeably surprised at the outcome.

Take a break

When people are overworked they tend to think longingly of their holidays, but often vacations are ruined because they can't say 'no' to their work. Many people find it hard to take a real break. They are incapable of turning off from the stimulus that comes from their business. Although they are on holiday, they clutch their laptops as they board the plane and while they are away check their emails daily, retrieve messages from their mobiles and talk to their secretaries, colleagues and superiors at the office.

This is no holiday. It's a continuation of their working lives carried on from another location! There's no stress busting going on here. By succumbing to the daily information glut emanating from their offices, they fail miserably in taking that well-earned rest and are not fully participating in the longed-for holiday.

If you are trying to manage your stress levels, it is vital to cut back drastically on the amount of communication with the office while you are away. It may not be possible to go completely 'cold turkey', but at least set some realistic boundaries. Make it clear to colleagues and associates that while they can remain in contact, communication should be kept to an absolute minimum.

Another important point to consider is why this vacation is important. What do you need from the trip? If you're on holiday with your family, what do they need from this trip? Are you going along to be a fully participating member of the group?

Remember, the best gift you can give anyone is the gift of time. Quality time with families and friends is important if you are to achieve a well-balanced life. If you block out sufficient time, at regular intervals, and schedule it to share with those closest to you, this can have a real impact. It makes for good, strong relationships from which everyone benefits.

If you want to use your holiday to catch up on reading, do confine it to what you *want* to read. While some people pack too many pairs of shoes and loads of clothes, my suitcases are always full of papers and books. They are, consequently, much heavier than the bags belonging to the rest of my family. I have often paid excess baggage fees for transporting tons of paper to sunny locations, never to get around to reading the contents!

An ideal holiday policy is to blank out completely. If you're gone, you're gone. No email, no phone, no work-related updates of any kind. For this to work really well, the holiday should be two weeks long. For most near-workaholics, the first few days are taken up unwinding completely. Your mind is still 'in the office'. The next two days you begin to relax. By the beginning of the second week you're on a different planet. When it's time to come home, you'll be almost excited at the prospect of returning to work!

Kickstart tip

Ignore holidays at your peril. Anyone who has a lot of responsibility needs to get away from the workplace for a period of time. It is a rejuvenating experience. More important, you're probably not the only one to benefit – your colleagues and staff deserve a break from you too!

It might be appropriate here to draw the distinction between trips and travelling. For most people taking a holiday means going on a trip. They know where they are going, they chosen the location, the amenities and surroundings. For it to be a success, it meets their expectations. If it falls short, it's a disappointment.

Travel, on the other hand, is not about such superficialities. Travelling is about seeing beneath the surface. It is about self-discovery.

In reality, cramming this into a two-week holiday is an impossibility. But if the opportunity were to present itself – say a three-month sabbatical, or a period of garden leave – wouldn't that be the perfect antidote to stress?

Creating personal reserves

Try to distance yourself from stress-inducing situations by creating personal reserves. Pacing yourself is one approach, if you have a number of difficult tasks ahead. Concentrate on one thing at a time.

Letting go of a situation is not failure. It is a positive and powerful course of action. In order to renew your energy and focus your attention, usually something has to be given up.

Do something relaxing. Creative ideas often come away from the work situation. The solution to a problem can appear if you allow your subconscious mind to operate.

Work on developing your instincts by using all your senses: seeing, hearing, feeling, taste and smell. Instincts are natural indicators if you are prepared to use them.

For more on dealing with stress, see *Kickstart Your Stress Management* in this series.

Summary

Ten steps to a healthier, less stressful life:

- Pay attention to health-related issues and stress symptoms.
- Define positive and negative stress situations that affect you.
- Check your individual stress levels and develop coping strategies.
- Use common sense.
- Look after your body.

- Control your mind.
- Keep an eye on your work/life balance.
- Be assertive – take control.
- Take a break.
- Create your own reserves – no one else can do it for you!

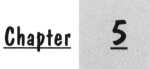

Chapter 5

Time Management in the Home

Three o'clock is always too late or too early for anything you want to do.

Jean-Paul Sartre, *La Nausée*

Before you skip this chapter thinking that it's only for people who don't go out to work, stop there! This chapter is for everyone. If you didn't work and have time management concerns, you wouldn't be reading this book. But you also have a home to go to at the end of the day. Whether the majority of your work is done in the office or in the home, the same issues stress you out and there are common themes to your days.

There are few people to whom these thoughts and suggestions don't apply. Whether you live alone with only a stick insect in a box for company, or share your life with a spouse, partner, children or others, there are messages here to help with time management issues outside the workplace.

Kickstart tip

If (with apologies to Rudyard Kipling)

If you can start the day without caffeine or pep pills
If you can be cheerful, ignoring aches and pains
If you can resist complaining and boring people with your troubles
If you can eat the same food every day and be grateful for it
If you can understand when loved ones are too busy to give you time
If you can overlook people taking things out on you when, through no fault of your own, things go wrong
If you can take criticism and blame without resentment
If you can face the world without lies and deceit
If you can conquer tension without medical help, relax without liquor and sleep without the aid of drugs
Then . . . you are probably either a cat or a dog

When did you last read a book?

You may work part of the time from home, on a remote basis, or in addition to a job have the responsibility of running a house with all its inherent management issues. Whatever the circumstances, you need lists as prompts and reminders of the task list for each day. Ideally before going to bed you should prepare your domestic to do list for the following day just as you would for the office. That way you can review and revise it in the morning.

A weekly list works well for some people: start the week with a new list of things to be achieved during that week. Allocate tasks to specific days and time slots during the week. If it is desk work, sit down with a list of five things to be achieved and don't leave until they are done. If they are all priority tasks, it is best not to let the list get longer than five things. Knowing that you will run out of time to get them done can be demoralizing. By not achieving what you set out to do you are setting unrealistic targets. Good time management is based on reality!

Your to do list, revised at breakfast time, should contain all the things you want to achieve in the day. As outlined in Chapter 3, spend a few minutes prioritizing and timetabling. First, block out a time of day for yourself – your quiet time.

The first hour of my day is spent in blissful isolation, before the rest of the family show any signs of waking. When emailing first became popular, friends and colleagues were aghast to see the time at which my messages were sent. 'Are you ill?', 'I didn't know you were an insomniac', 'No normal person gets up that early in the morning!' were just a few of the remarks I received. I am now a much more cautious emailer and leave the messages in the 'To be sent later' file, pressing the button at around 8.30am so as not to frighten people.

Kickstart tip

To be able to look after others, you first need to look after yourself.

Meeting the demands of domestic life

Another quote from Og Mandino:

> Never again clutter your days or nights with so many menial and unimportant things that you have no time to accept a real challenge when it comes along. This applies to play as well as work. A day merely survived is no cause for celebration. You are not here to fritter away your precious hours when you have the ability to accomplish so much by making a slight change in your routine. No more busy work. No more hiding from success. Leave time, leave space, to grow. Now. Now! Not tomorrow!

The other week I had a call from a work colleague. 'What are you doing?' I asked.

'I'm house managing for a week,' he replied proudly. 'While my wife's away with her mother, I said I'd mind the children and work from home. I'm going to catch up on my office work and work through the list of jobs that have been left for me to do.'

At the office this person is known to have a large cardboard box into which he puts all mail addressed solely to him. His secretary goes through it about once a fortnight, chucks out all the junk mail, sorts his correspondence and identifies the letters that are really important.

His secretary and his wife are in frequent contact. They both know who they have to deal with. Both make lists, endless lists. The company in which he works is large and there is plenty of back-up and support staff. At home his wife gets as many people to help on the home front as possible – cleaner, gardener, someone to do ironing etc. Nothing very innovative, but it seems to work.

It was Wednesday morning when I heard how my colleague was getting on. He'd asked his secretary to come over and help him with his office work and she'd ended up sorting out the domestic situation as well!

We may not all be so fortunate to have people on hand to sort things for us. If you have to do most things yourself because you don't have a huge team of perfectly trained staff running around after you, here are some ideas for busy people who also have work to do at home.

Kickstart tip

If you combine working with running a home you may not live alone. To make life easier, adopt the following house rules:

If you take it out – put it back
If you open it – close it
If you throw it down – pick it up again
If you take something off – hang it up

One simple but effective resolution to which a friend of mine sticks is that when going out, she makes a route so that she doesn't end up back-tracking on herself. If she can, she walks or cycles into town. This gets her exercise schedule done without having to set other time aside to do it.

Guard against getting waylaid by B list tasks when at home. Particularly if Saturdays and Sundays are the only full days you spend at home, you should aim to plan the day and work out how much time you need to spend on certain tasks. If you have to tackle big tasks or difficult problems, spend at least a part of your day thinking about them or doing part of them. This makes the going easier.

Make sure that at the end of each day you review your task list to see what's left. Also make sure that tomorrow's A list tasks are realistic and reallocate non-core tasks when planning the new day.

If part of your work is looking after others, how can you do this if you don't look after yourself? From recent research I have found out that members of the clergy are told at the beginning of each year to book up their annual retreats as the No. 1 priority. They are not expected to look after others spiritually if they don't get their own 'fix'.

For us the equivalent is holidays. Obviously we have to be careful about when we go away, but having booked the time everything needs to work around those dates. You should never interrupt a holiday. That's why it's best to be incommunicado while away on vacation, as discussed in Chapter 4. Stick to the dates and things either wait or get on perfectly well without us.

When having time off, avoid people who remind you of work. It's a sad fact that few people actually enjoy time off if they spend it in or near their known work environment. It is important to have a part of your life that has nothing to do with your job.

Reading days are refreshing for many people, and essential for others if they are to keep up with trends and developments in their professions. A day a month should be sufficient, but do block it out in the calendar. If you are able to organize this, it is a good day to spend at home. But remember to avoid interruptions. I reserve my reading time for train travel. I spend about six hours a week travelling and it is an excellent time for catching up with reports, press articles and journals.

Kickstart tip

If you are having difficulty scheduling your time for optimum output because you are not dominated by office hours, try the cloverleaf approach. Divide the day into three parts. Work two out of every three – i.e. if you know you have a heavy evening, don't work either the morning or the afternoon. If that's not particularly easy, try changing the type of work you do at those times.

For example, get paperwork done swiftly if you have been out on visits or attending meetings. Always plan in advance for maximum results. Don't be persuaded that housework, DIY and gardening aren't work – they are! Homes require maintenance and if you didn't do it, you'd be paying someone else to do it for you. In any case, it's a valid investment of your time to keep your main assets in good repair.

Most people work to deadlines set by others, but you can also set them for yourself. You can, for example, make a date with yourself to do your tax or VAT return, before the reminder hit your desk. Or make a date to go through your filing cabinet or the cupboard under the stairs.

Setting aside one day a month for administrative tasks helps make sure that you keep up to date with paperwork – paying bills, expenses etc. Put the date in the diary and arrange for a treat at the end as a reward – it is otherwise such a dreary way to spend your time. If you are efficient and doing it regularly, the situation does not get out of hand. The prospect of a trip to the cinema or a meal out helps with motivation throughout the day.

One of the biggest challenges for time management when working independently is being disciplined enough to get things done when there are no external deadlines driving you. It is so easy to get distracted by lots of administrative trivia. You are easily able to justify the time by saying you are doing 'something' while deferring the big or difficult tasks that should really be tackled.

If this sounds familiar, try writing things that need to be done on a piece of paper and sticking it on the fridge so that it is always visible to you and anyone else who comes into range. As discussed before, it's harder to avoid doing something once you've gone public on your commitment. (It isn't always infallible but it does help.) Don't rely solely on sticky notes – they can fall off and lie unseen underneath the fridge for years!

If there's a really tight deadline (and this applies equally well to working in the office as well as at home) and work needs to be done, I put the voicemail on and don't go near my emails. Every four hours I quickly check emails and messages for anything urgent. Other than that, I just ignore the incoming stuff until the task in hand is completed.

Meetings not conducted in an office location are often seen by others as having less strict time restraints. It is important for home-workers who make dates with people to come and talk to give clear indicators in terms of time. 'We have exactly one hour and I'm going to have to be very strict', for example. If people know the boundaries, they are more likely to respect them. After all, just because you are not sitting in the office does not mean that your time isn't valuable.

Be tough – don't let someone drop a bombshell on you while standing on your doorstep at the point of departure. Explain politely that you're sorry they didn't mention this earlier, it will have to wait. They'll soon learn. Somehow it's easier to be taken advantage of when working with non-business/non-professional people who assume that because you're at home you must be on holiday or have no work to do. If only they knew!

An anecdote attributed to Mark Twain goes something like this: whenever anyone rang his doorbell, he would put on his coat. On opening the door, if the caller was welcome he would say, 'How lucky you are to catch me, I have just come in.' If the caller was not welcome, he would say how sorry he was he couldn't stop, but he was on his way out.

In summer time, or if adapting this trick to work in the office, just grab a bag or file of papers and look purposeful.

Kickstart tip

Every now and again, make a weekly, monthly or yearly timetable to see where the time goes. Then try adjusting the balance!

Spend one day a week doing something different. For some people this might be charity work or volunteering for a service-based task. It puts a different focus on life and produces a feel-good factor. I really enjoy this part of my week.

Life is too short to stuff a mushroom.

Shirley Conran, *Down with Superwoman*

Thinking about that often-used quotation, it struck me that there is too much that is interesting in life to make the simple complex! I am happy chopping and frying the mushrooms, thus leaving more time for richer pursuits.

When you are short of time, you need to develop an ability to ditch or delegate tasks. This is as relevant at home as at the office.

Clutter clearance

Have nothing in your home that you do not know to be useful and believe to be beautiful.

William Morris

One way to improve your time management is to simplify the amount of things you have to do. Cut down on the amount of time spent getting ready in the morning by having clothes ready, shirts ironed etc. the night before. Keep your personal grooming routine simple and low maintenance.

Be drastic when sorting through cupboards and drawers. Clear out unwanted items. Organize them and keep them tidy. This saves a huge amount of time that would otherwise be spent searching – it takes no time at all to find anything if it's in the right place.

Cut down on paperwork. Simplify administrative tasks as much as possible. Do personal writing jobs at unsociable times when you can't use the phone. If you're particularly busy, get help with these chores to maximize the use of your time at weekends.

Use your designated reading time for all those piled-up articles – at the end of the time ditch them, even if they're still unread. Be ruthless!

Make sure to spend time each month reviewing and evaluating how you spend your time.

Stop trying to prove you're perfect

Keep a contact list

Another way to help yourself on the domestic front is to develop relationships with shops and service providers locally or via the internet. By making a list of contacts you can turn to when you are short of time and have something that needs to be done, you don't get stressed out doing it yourself.

If your network of local service providers actually consists of a drawer full of bits of paper plus one or two out-of-date local directories, get started on creating your own database/directory.

My contact list has been compiled over a number of years. It expands on a daily or weekly basis. I use part of my admin time to add or delete people from it and update it on a weekly basis. It is backed up on the computer so that if my handheld device is lost or stolen, the data is instantly retrievable.

Names should be deleted if the people are no longer relevant, particularly after a house move that could mean you are no longer local to those suppliers, in which case the new local shops should be substituted. The list should include everything from your accountant to the local zoo (and mine does)!

With a reputable and dependable support network, you will find it possible to get more done – particularly when coping with the demands of a job and running a home.

If you have the technology, put everything on your PC and use a handheld computer. It's also well worth spending a little time working out a sensible system of categories. They need to be fairly accurate to be useful, yet easily retrievable by others as well as yourself.

I wish I had a pound for each time a member of my family goes to look for something I've requested and comes back with the answer, 'It's not there'. There's no point in listing 'Patty', the greatest dressmaker in the world, under 'School' just because you remember that's where you first met. Although you know that, it's doubtful that your nearest and dearest will!

Service providers should be distinguished between work/professional and domestic. There's nothing worse than wasting precious minutes hunting for the bank manager or new accountant's details among lots of clothes shops, cleaners, taxis and the local delicatessen. Cross-referencing is important too. Spend a bit of time working out when and how you'll want to retrieve these details and it will save you hours in future.

Flexibility

Kickstart tip

Remember you can choose the way you respond to people and events. If you consciously replace the words 'I have to' with 'I've decided to', every action in life becomes a choice that you have freely made. Decisions are one of the strongest tools towards achieving successful time management.

The ability to be flexible is vital to anyone who has time constraints in their life. Being able to think 'outside the box', whether at work or at home, and keeping an open mind are vital skills. Making measured and sensible decisions is so important. Keeping an up-beat and positive attitude also helps. Laughing instead of crying is easier and much better for you – particularly when things get really wild and crazy.

Crises do happen and the clever ones among us allow for the unexpected. Someone will phone in distress or depression and need a shoulder to cry on. This is where 'flexi-hour' thinking comes into play. If you are sufficiently organized to have a 'buffer' zone, you can give the time needed and not over-stretch yourself.

Kickstart tip

To be in control of your mind, you need to set aside 30 minutes each day for yourself alone. Use this half-hour for introspection by asking yourself, 'How can I respond more effectively to my challenges?'

A friend of mine who works from home and is an entrepreneur *extraordinaire* confessed, 'My time management is a sort of on–off affair, and mainly the latter! I try to keep healthy, calm and tidy. I attempt to delegate anything and everything that is possible so that I can keep my time for creative thought.'

One suggestion she offered was to use a kitchen timer to help get rid of irksome tasks that everyone tries to avoid doing. Set the pinger for a length of time and don't work beyond that at the particular task. This is very useful when doing things you dislike as you can be pleasantly surprised how short a time they take to do. It is also extraordinarily simple bearing in mind how much time you may have wasted putting the task off and/or worrying about it.

The timer idea is also useful for avoiding spending too much time on something. When you enjoy doing a job, it is so easy to carry on over-doing it way beyond the time required. This is one of my particular faults.

Avoid exploitation – lighten the load

Using the home as a workplace can have its advantages. For a while some years ago I worked from home as a virtual assistant. At the time I was doing a lot of work for two clients who lived abroad, one in Texas and the other in Dubai. Between them the phones started ringing as early as 5 am (from Dubai) and finished around 11 pm (in Texas). It might not be to everyone's taste to be at work something approaching 18 hours a day, but it had practical advantages.

Although my work was generated over an 18-hour day, I was able to take breaks. I dealt with domestic tasks and worked for UK clients in the intervening time. Since the majority of the overseas clients' work could be done by email, fax or telephone, neither of these clients had to see me looking presentable. I was just out of bed when dealing with the Dubai client and was often in my dressing gown when talking to my client in Texas.

Use the machinery to take the strain. Let the answerphone screen calls while you deal with a situation that demands your more immediate attention. It is easy enough to return the call later and explain to the caller, if required, that you were engaged on the other line.

Many years ago I took advantage of my unusual work schedule to boost our business. When my second child was just a few weeks old we had dealings with clients in New Zealand. Because of the huge time difference (something approaching 12 hours), the ideal time to speak to them was about 3 am. The clients were hugely impressed with our dedication to their needs. 'You called us specially, how very good of you!' They had no idea that my schedule of night feeds ensured I was wide awake at that time. It made perfect use of the time and generated a good working relationship and profitable sales.

One thing you can't recycle is wasted time.

When you have a lot to cope with, it is good to try to be a swan. If people say 'you never look busy', take that as a compliment and be thankful that they cannot see beneath the waterline at the frantic paddling going on!

It is possible that managing time, all the time, can be counterproductive. It always intrigues me to read reports in the press about the life of business tycoons (men or women) who get up at 6.30 am and by 7.15 have showered, breakfasted, got to the office, scanned the papers and done 100 push-ups! The answer to their time management skills probably lies in the words wife, housekeeper, chauffeur, PA and being extremely difficult . . .

Summary

- Become a list freak! List all the things you have to do. Once something has been carried forward five times, cross it out – you'll probably never do it anyway.
- Start the day by doing the job you hate most, just to get it out of the way.
- Work on your personal network of other people who can do everything that takes up your valuable time, such as shopping. You don't have to be perfect.
- Consider how you spend your time – even though you've always done something, is it still valid?
- If you look after others, make sure you take care of yourself.
- Simplify life – get rid of clutter – use whatever it takes.
- Be flexible – avoid over-doing things and enjoy the slack.

Chapter **6**

Time Management at Work

No one on their deathbed said, 'I wish I'd spent more time in the office.'

Anon.

If you count the number of times you leave the office with important work unfinished, wondering where the day went, the question you need to ask yourself is, 'What really happened to my time?' Until you know where your time goes, you can't really start to control it, manage it or organize it.

Consider this scenario: 'Yesterday at 9 am as I walk to my desk my assistant stops me and gives me the latest details on a project. This impromptu report goes on and on. Then the telephone interrupts us. My PA tells me she will come back to me later and goes off to deal with the call.

'Meanwhile I start work. I dive straight into the first 'must do' on my list. It's a long and complex proposal and needs careful thought. There's a paper relating to it that I must read first. I *know* it was on my desk last week, and it was definitely there on Monday. I spend ten minutes looking for it.

'In the middle of my search, I'm interrupted by a phone call, neither urgent nor important, asking for my opinion about a competitor. I'm just about to make a new start on the proposal when my PA turns up at my desk to continue the discussion we started earlier! The phone rings again. This time it's the printer wanting to discuss the final proofs of our new brochure, copies of which he's just emailed over.

'The PA leaves the room while I spend half an hour on the phone with the printer. It's now nearly midday and I haven't even started on my 'must do' list. What's wrong? Why aren't I getting things done? I've made my lists and it's not working!'

Thinking about this executive's dilemma, it was clear that the problem lay with him. People behaved like this because he let them and because he didn't give them any other outlet. He needed to be able to handle his day better. Maybe he should delegate to his staff in writing, giving a due date, and manage by exception. He should only allow his staff to tell him significant things that are not going to plan, not the things that are going well, then he can stop getting hijacked.

Kickstart tip

You may have the intention, but do you pay the attention?

I suggest that when thinking about your time management at work, you start by keeping a diary, or a time sheet, to record your daily activities for a week (see Figure 6.1 on page 96). It is amazing what surprises this reveals. The two things to remember are to account for every minute of the day and not to cheat. Put down everything you do, from going to buy a coffee to a quick phone call home.

Once the information is available, analyse the results to find out where the 'time bandits' are. These are the activities that seriously divert you from your work.

The Four 'Time Bandits' are close relatives of the Four Horsemen of the Apocalypse. If allowed to have free rein, they can make you feel hunted. They are in order of popularity:

1 **Disorganization** – untidy desk and unworkable systems, i.e. lack of filing.
2 **Interruptions** – unexpected telephone calls and unsolicited visitors.
3 **Invitations and requests** – meetings, conferences, seminars and other time-consuming tasks.
4 **Paperwork** – urgent and important to others, which you had relegated to be dealt with later.

Organization in the office

> I've developed a new philosophy . . . I only dread one day at a time.
>
> Charlie Brown

When faced with an impossibly busy schedule, the first and foremost tip for anyone is to get and keep organized at all times. Organization is the key to a successful working life, whether it is the relationship between a secretary and a boss, a manager and a director, or any other working association.

One reason some people are unable to cope with their work is that they do not like it and cannot face it. No amount of organization is ever going to help here. If you know someone in this position, suggest they take a deep breath and try to get back into it, or look for something different to do, possibly consider other jobs within your organization or a change of direction.

How much time did you spend …	Time spent		Action that can be taken to review/ change the situation
	hrs/mins	% of total	
1. Anticipation and pre-planning? … dealing with things that were unexpected? … dealing with things that you expected or had anticipated but for which you had made no preparations? … dealing with things that you had expected, thought about and for which you made some tangible preparations and plans?			
2. Sources of demands … responding to the demands of your immediate boss or of other senior people? … responding to the demands of colleagues on the same level as yourself? … responding to the demands of your immediate subordinates and other 'junior' staff? … responding to the demands of the 'system'?			
3. Contacts … on your own? … with your immediate subordinates? … with your immediate boss? … with other people?			
4. Location … in your own 'office'? … in other people's 'offices'? … on sites and plants? … travelling? … other?			
5. Paperwork … handling paperwork? … writing/reading letters and memos? … dealing with other paperwork?			
6. Urgency and crises … dealing with issues that were urgent? … dealing with things that were urgent but not important?			
7. Specialist & managerial activities … dealing with specialist matters for which you were trained … dealing with managerial issues not immediately connected with people? … dealing with people management issues (i.e. recruiting, disciplinary, training, counselling, supporting, directing, leading etc.)? … dealing with organizational and procedural administration?			
8. Personal areas … on things of largely personal interest (incl. meetings that, whether you went or not, depended solely on you)? … on coffee and meal breaks and other breaks for personal needs? … training, educating or developing yourself? … on social activities made necessary by the job?			
9. Other aspects of importance to you			

Figure 6.1   Sample analysis sheet

Anticipate that need

Organized people are able to put their hands on whatever is needed before a superior or colleague has even thought about requesting it. When arriving at work, open up the office/work station and turn on the computer so that by the time you're ready to sit down, you can get straight on with your work.

Do whatever it takes to make your own day (and that of your boss, if you have one) go as smoothly as possible. Pre-empt and put out any fires while they are still wisps of smoke!

Kickstart tip

If you don't take control of your time, someone else is likely to do it for you.

Most of the time, disorganized superiors or colleagues do not have a clue what organized people do to make working days run smoothly. This applies equally at home and out of office situations. If you rise early, try getting to work before anyone else. It allows you time to get oriented and prepared for the day.

It's a good idea to cushion your time schedules. The organized person always builds in time for travel. Whether it is getting to work or travelling to and from appointments, this can get overlooked, particularly when the meeting is nearby. By not allowing for travelling time you can be late for the next appointment and end up failing to keep to your schedule.

First things first

Kickstart tip

On the way to work, visualize exactly what you are going to do.

Always start by checking your calendar/diary/daily schedule. This is your bible. All dates, times, events and tasks to be done should be listed for each day. Review it throughout the day to make sure that nothing gets overlooked. As soon as other people arrive and start asking for things to be done, rescheduling may be required. Keep up with them by filling in these appointments immediately or making the necessary changes. Advise those concerned, at once, if there are clashes. Appointments may have to be rescheduled or cancelled in the light of unavoidable developments.

Lists again!

Make a list last thing before leaving the office of *everything* that is outstanding. Note exactly where you have left the last unfinished job. List it all – not just the jobs you need to get done the following day. Briefly consider the next day's agenda. This clears your mind and enables you to leave work issues behind (with your list) on your desk overnight. Mark the first three things you are going to do, in order of priority, the following day.

On reaching your desk the next morning, do the first task *before* checking the answerphone, emails, post etc. Then there is no time wasted deciding where to start, sharpening pencils etc. Once work has begun it seems to go on more easily from there.

Don't cherry pick

Kickstart tip

Always make the first job worthwhile. 'Seize the day before it flies away.'

So start each day by doing a key task. Get the difficult tasks done quickly. Avoid the 'dread' factor. It makes you feel better to have something done and dusted. The most effective people deal with problems before they become crises. If you can get the tricky issues handled in the early part of the day, it makes the rest of the time far more enjoyable. Establish a reward system for difficult jobs done – take a break or have a snack.

If a job is particularly unpleasant or difficult, make it routine. Then you don't have to think about its complexity or unattractiveness. Backing it up with an even more unappealing task can force you to do it out of choice. Try 'chunking' it – spend 15 minutes on it first thing in the morning. You can put up with almost anything provided you know there's a time limit. If you make this automatic, you will have broken through the pain barrier.

Most stress and fatigue are caused not by working, but by worrying about the things you didn't do. Once you've accomplished your difficult task, you enjoy the rest of the working day. You go home feeling happier and more motivated and end up having a better evening. You even feel fresher for the next day. This may sound simple, but it works.

Dealing with interruptions

> Until we value ourselves, we won't value our time. Until we value our time, we won't do anything with it.
>
> M. Scott Peck

The more you allow yourself to be interrupted, the more interruptions you'll get.

To avoid getting sidetracked by interruptions, look for ways to bunch them together. Once you've dealt with them, immediately get back to the main task for the day.

Pre-empting interruptions

You can pre-empt interruptions by giving advance warning to others. Telling colleagues that you don't want to be disturbed puts them 'on notice' that you're not prepared to take unsolicited visits or calls and is well worth practising. Advising them of the project you're working on can avoid frustration later. There is nothing worse than spending hours preparing work only to be given some additional data at a later stage that alters the whole project so drastically that the job has to be redone almost from scratch.

Don't encourage interruptions – close doors, focus on the work in hand. Telling people that you're 'in a meeting' is often all that is needed for you to be left alone. There's no need to admit that you're actually in a meeting with yourself! If this is what it takes to buy you some quiet time to get on with an important job, just do it. Most people are conditioned to back off when told that someone is in a meeting.

Refusing interruptions

Hang a 'do not disturb' sign on your door. Go and work in the car, use an unoccupied meeting room, or work from someone else's office. Be proactive and assertive. When an interruption occurs, slot it into your priority list. If the client's call is related to a task at the bottom of the list (one of the ten jobs on today's to do list), ask if they can be rung back later that afternoon. Should another interruption fall into the 'urgent and important' bracket, you may need to be flexible enough to 'down tools' and help. Not taking action may have implications for the rest of your working week.

Do be prepared to say 'No'. Be pleasant but firm and don't offer reasons. It is always helpful to say when you will be available, however.

Managing interruptions

People who like to be liked find it far harder to resist interruptions. Good relationships with colleagues and staff can sometimes come at a price! You can easily get ambushed because you don't like saying no. To help manage interruptions, you need to work out who needs access to you at given times. Issue clear guidelines as to who, when and why you can be interrupted. Otherwise let the machines take the strain, or a colleague (if you are prepared to return the favour).

If someone gets through your door, ask them why they have come to see you. Don't let them settle in. Stand up when they enter the office and then perch on the edge of the desk. Beware of small talk – save that for the pub or coffee break. Be ruthless with time but gracious with people.

If someone insists on seeing you, agree to meet on their territory. That way you retain control of when you see them – and it's much easier to leave. If time runs out and the matter cannot be sorted, close down the conversation by suggesting another meeting at a more convenient time.

Telephone interruptions

Kickstart tip

The best time to call people is either before 9 am – but not too early! – or after 4 pm, because these are outside normal meeting hours.

Set aside time each day for priority work, which means time when you don't accept calls. Field the calls by diverting them to someone, if that's possible. Otherwise switch to voicemail and leave a message telling people the best time of day to call when you will be available to speak to them. Call them back at a better time but be courteous – ask if the time is convenient for them.

Make telephone calls in blocks, at the most appropriate time. Limit this to one or two periods a day. List the number of calls you need to make. Always have a note of the objectives of each call and include the main points you want to raise – don't waffle. Keep a timer handy so that you remain aware of the time passing while on the phone.

When you leave a voice message, don't merely leave your name and a request that the person calls you. Explain why you are calling and what you need to know. That gives the other person time to research the answer before calling you back. It also increases the likelihood that they will return your call.

People who interrupt

Kickstart tip

Whenever you are pressed for time, always stand. Don't offer or accept an invitation to sit down. Carrying papers indicates that you have another appointment.

Try replacing an 'open door' policy with a 'visiting hour'. With a little persuasion it may be possible to steer people towards visits by appointment only. If you are prepared to reciprocate, this can work well. Try treating others the way you would like to be treated yourself. Always check with colleagues if they are happy to accept drop-in visits.

For anyone who needs to maximize the use of their working day, one strategy is dealing pleasantly but firmly with unsolicited visitors. When under pressure this requires tact and diplomacy. By all means be assertive – don't be manipulated. If the other person's call on your time is not urgent, suggest fixing a meeting at a later date that is mutually convenient.

Other assertive reactions to interruptions from others include honesty and fairness. By acknowledging your gut reactions, feelings and wants, you also accept that others have an equal right to their feelings and needs. Aim to judge each situation on its own merits.

Requests and invitations

The key here is knowing what you need to do, rather than what you would like to do (if time permits). Ask yourself whether someone else could attend a meeting or event on your behalf and get the same result. What would be the benefit if you accepted? Networking is an important and valuable skill, and if opportunities arise they should not be passed over.

If there is no discernible advantage to your attending a function, other than out of politeness or a sense of duty, then decline. If you are declining then say 'No', clearly and directly, without feeling the need to apologize or make excuses. You can use the same approach when you want to shift the deadline for a piece of time-sensitive work.

If you are asked for an immediate response to a query, you can ask why respectfully and politely. Perhaps the enquirer's deadline is driven by a misunderstanding?

Remember to reject the request, not the person. Explain if you feel it necessary and acknowledge the feelings involved. Watch that your body language doesn't contradict what you're saying.

If you are undecided, say so and ask for more time or information. Don't forget, if you can't say 'No', what is the value of your 'Yes'?

Paperwork

Keep a tidy desk at all times. That is easy to say, but it is a real challenge for people who find paperwork and admin tasks tedious. These jobs are often postponed while you carry on with more enjoyable (and often less important) tasks. But if you can get into the habit of dealing with the tasks you hate as early as possible in the day, the sense of achievement is huge. It is so satisfying to be able to cross the nagging job off your to do list.

When faced with piles of paperwork, be ruthless and deal with a piece of paper only once. If appropriate, deal with paperwork on a daily basis. This way it may only take up 10–20 minutes of your time. If your desk remains clear and uncluttered, work will go more smoothly (see Chapter 8).

Systems

Do you have the right systems in place? These need not be complicated to be effective. Information management and filing must be done regularly. Set aside a day each week for admin tasks – say Friday afternoon and Monday morning. Keep the systems simple but memorable. The skill of filing paper lies in its ease of retrieval.

I recommend a system that is kept in sync with your diary. In my desk drawer are 43 files – one for each day of the month, and one for each month of the year. For example, in April if the diary has an entry saying '21/4 – write proposal for X', under file 21 is all the material needed to do it (see Chapter 8 again).

If you don't have methods to help you work, how can you achieve your goals and targets? Set realistic deadlines. Be conscious of time – and always allow a little more than you think you'll need.

The importance of saying 'No'

We've already touched on this, but it is so important that here it is again.

Everyone wants their work to matter, but sometimes they allow it to matter too much. If you think that by giving more than 100 per cent of yourself to your job you are adding value, you are wrong. Of course you want to feel valued and appreciated at work. But if you rely on work for a sense of self-worth, by working harder and longer and never saying no, then you need to re-evaluate what you do and how long you spend doing it.

If you are overwhelmed by work, you have to begin to say no. Until you do that, no amount of problem solving, motivation, time management or working smarter will help. When you are overloaded with work you have to acknowledge that there are some things you don't want to do, and some things that you simply cannot do. Be honest and say so. Real assertiveness is required here! Sometimes the jobs you're asked to complete aren't even yours. Practise saying no to these first.

For example, the busier you are, the greater the number of telephone calls and emails you tend to receive. Some of these calls and emails will require an urgent response. How do you develop the skills to cope with this?

Remember that sometimes you need to learn to work S M A R T:

S *specific* – do you know what you want to achieve?
M *measurable* – do you have an idea how much use it will be?
A *achievable* – are you sure you are really able to tackle it?
R *relevant* – does it really matter?
T *time based* – how long is it going to take?

If you have access to a PA or other help, have him or her screen your calls and emails. Only the urgent ones need to be forwarded. The rest can wait until your 'admin' day.

Set aside time to have appointments with yourself. Agree with colleagues when it is best to have 'quiet time'. Sometimes entire departments agree on an hour (usually first thing in the morning) when everyone works quietly without interrupting anyone else.

Blocking out part of the day for private or 'thinking time' is both positive and helpful. Most of us get more done then than in a whole day full of interruptions. You can use this time effectively to decide when to say no and when to say yes. This gives you space to work out realistic deadlines. If you set aside time to plan, you can deal with work more quickly and avoid being overwhelmed.

Planning

The shortest way to do many things is to do only one thing at once.

Samuel Smiles (1812–1904)

Failing to plan is planning to fail. All good time managers plan effectively. This applies equally to your private as well as to your working life. The main criteria for good planning include goals, lists, priorities, concentration and urgency.

To plan effectively you need to set out in detail how you intend to achieve your goals. Goals should be specific and measurable, Measurement of goals can often be achieved by making them time oriented. This should include timescale, deadlines, tasks involved, people to contact and resources required.

Then you need to be able to distinguish between 'progress tasks' and 'maintenance tasks'.

- A *progress* task is one that you believe will move you towards a position better than the one you are in now.
- A *maintenance* task is one that allows you to move to a position equivalent to one you have been in before.

Planning – long-term overview

To be organized in the office it helps to have a strategic plan. Identify your goals in relation to the company's objectives. When establishing your priorities, list all the tasks involved in achieving those goals. Then review the plan, streamline it, put it into practice, evaluate it and add new goals! This plan should be kept and reviewed every six months.

Planning – mid-term

In relation to the long-term plan, establish medium-term priorities in terms of urgency and importance. Delegate where possible. Allocate tasks to suitable times and set deadlines to complete tasks. Break down complex tasks into more manageable sub-activities. Review these against the long-term plan, say every three months.

Planning – weekly

At the end of each week, allocate time to write out your weekly action list. This is a visible collection of important tasks to be accomplished during the coming week. When sitting down to plan your time, block out the amount needed in your schedule.

Planning – day-to-day basis

Identify your tasks in order of importance and urgency. Always number and prioritize items on the to do list. Don't underestimate time or overload yourself. Allow for the fact that there will be phone calls and interruptions by giving yourself extra time for each item. You should not commit more than 60 per cent of your day.

Allowing for 'slack time' in your daily schedule helps you to cope with the unexpected. It also helps you to avoid falling into the 'over-scheduled' trap. Meetings do over-run, interruptions will happen and projects do take longer than anticipated. 'Over-scheduling' yourself is self-defeating.

Make it a rule to finish one task before starting the next one and allow yourself the satisfaction of crossing each job off when completed. Set deadlines and try hard not to be distracted by other issues that come up during the day.

By always giving a date and approximate time when you will get back to someone who needs your attention, you are being assertive and proactive. If the problem is urgent and time critical, reviewing your 'today' list is essential. You should be able to see what can be moved to the following day. Once the day is over, always put the items that are not crossed off on to the next day's list. Prioritize these first.

Use the following priorities (Figure 6.2):

A **Important and urgent** – quality issues, quality time, do today.
B **Important but less urgent/immediate** – requiring quality time at a later date. People like to avoid these tasks for as long as possible. Split into shorter tasks and programme them in.
C **Urgent** – requiring a quick response, but often of little importance to objectives. Avoid them by effective planning, do or delegate.
D **Other** – don't require immediate action, no value towards objectives. Avoid or delegate.

The ratio of effort to time

It is worth mentioning here that the more effort spent on a project in its early stages, the greater the amount of time saved at the end. Early preparation in a project leads to better organization, better payback. It avoids blame, recrimination and litigation. Plan to work hard at the beginning of a new piece of work, so that the greatest input is early on. As time progresses, the amount of effort decreases rather than the other way round.

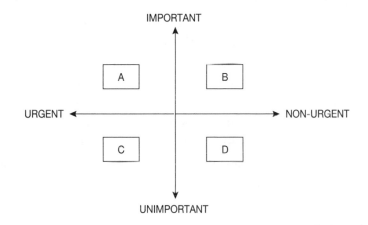

Figure 6.2   Important/urgent ratio

Time is money, or is it?

What is your time worth? Carry out this simple exercise. Start with your salary. Divide by the number of weeks worked. Then divide by the number of hours worked each week. Finally, divide by 60. That gives you the rate per minute for your time – your time is your most valuable commodity.

Time is not only money; employer or client satisfaction is what generates your income. If your aim is to make money, grade each task according to how much money it's going to earn you. Delegate tasks that have to be done but have a lower value.

Your success at work is directly related to the relationships you have with your employers and clients. It is not possible to have excellent relationships with everyone, but it is helpful to prioritize relationships, as well as tasks. For more on career success, see *Kickstart Your Career* in this series.

It may not simply be a matter of money. By using an imaginary currency to cost each of your tasks according to their value in meeting your objectives, you can see where they appear, then list them in order of priority.

Summary

Top ten time wasters at work:

- Interruptions – pre-empt them.
- Telephone – avoid windbags and waiting.
- Visitors – be ruthless with your time but polite with people.
- Paperwork – control excessive bureaucracy.
- Requests and invitations – rule out unnecessary activities.
- Inability to say 'no' – how can you value your 'yes'?
- Availability – build in some boundaries.
- Bad organization – tidy that desk so you don't waste ages looking for stuff.
- Lack of planning – without a plan you can't make the most of your time.
- Slack time – socializing should be built into non-prime time.

Chapter 7

Time Management and People: Clients, Staff, Friends and Family

I don't know the key to success, but the key to failure is to try to please everyone.

Bill Cosby

There is no doubt that relationships do matter. In connection with time management poor working relationships can cost companies huge amounts of time and money. Whether you are a manager or a subordinate, the best working relationships create optimum job performance.

Being a good boss is not necessarily a natural gift; much of what goes into being an effective manager is learned behaviour. There are some people who have a flawless touch with others and inspire, motivate and encourage them. Some people are gifted communicators and are people rather than task oriented. But for every natural there are just as many excellent communicators who got that way by attending courses and seminars and reading books on effective management.

Without clear communication, whether at work or at home, you can waste huge amounts of time correcting mistakes, waiting for other people's work, sitting for hours in irrelevant meetings and attempting to unravel confused lines of responsibility or authority. This leads to ineffective delegation and unnecessary checking, and plunges you into tasks without planning and adequate focus.

Good communicators understand people and that skill makes for easier relationships with others. In the office a successful team leader keeps staff motivated and focused. People can develop the capability to communicate well by mixing with others who have that ability. Communicating so that you are understood is only the start. Being understood and understanding others aren't enough either. The essential ingredient of good communication is building relationships.

Try to create a whole network of people in which everyone understands one another and takes suitable action.

This chapter considers briefly what bosses expect from staff and why staff sometimes fail to deliver, as well as the importance of making it clear to staff how you want them to perform. Obviously, if you don't have staff at the moment you can skip the chapter, but when you become a manager it may prove useful.

Why is this relevant to time management? The answer is simple – if you have people working for you, it is because you need them to help you achieve your objectives. Without them you will fail. The presence of staff is meant to reduce your workload, not increase it, and to maximize the most appropriate use of your time. If managed correctly your staff will enable you to achieve far more than you could possibly do alone.

Conversely, if you have a boss, good communication will help you to ensure that you make a good job of managing the time you have with your superior. For example, if your superior is never available, it may be that he or she is constantly required in meetings, or is unpunctual, inefficient or has poor personal organizational skills. Major problems can occur and will remain unresolved until he or she returns.

If your boss is unable or unwilling to communicate, this can lead to mistakes being made. Because you learn about policy or system changes by accident (after having wasted valuable time and effort producing unnecessary work) you are then chastised by your superior, who thought you should have known about them anyway.

Beware managers who change their mind. Sometimes a chance remark can spark off a flurry of irrelevant activity by staff, who move in confused and uncertain directions, thus wasting time on abortive projects.

> Communicative behaviour does not occur within a network of relationships but *is* that network.
>
> Leonard C. Hawes

Positive, productive relationships are easy to spot because people get on with each other, enjoy being together and react willingly when asked to carry out favours without expecting an immediate reward. People are trusting and share information and contacts readily.

Creating an environment of integrity, trust and respect requires making certain that everyone is treated fairly. Being inclusive keeps everyone up to speed when it comes to the company's aims and objectives.

Communicating effectively

It can be helpful to think of people as falling into one of four time styles (Figure 7.1).

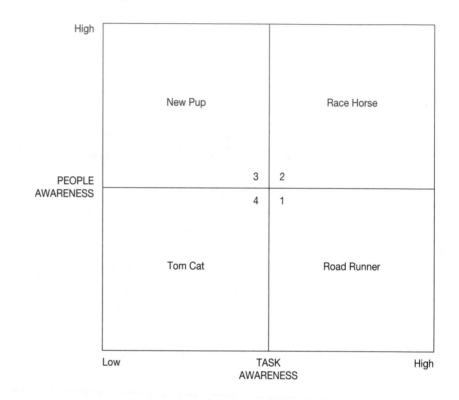

Figure 7.1   Time style awareness: people and tasks

Type 1   Road Runner

Road Runners like to get things done in a hurry. They have little time to talk to others and have a high awareness of time and getting the task done. The bottom line is important to them, even if they have to run over others to achieve it. They have a tendency to try to do the task by themselves. Their time management can sometimes turn into a crisis.

Type 2   Race Horse

Race Horses like to get things done in a hurry and ask others to help. Teamwork is important to them. They like to see others as part of the team and pulling their weight. They get a great sense of accomplishment when working with others and produce excellent results. They use people and tasks to meet time deadlines.

Type 3   New Pup

New Pups like people and time is measured by being with others. Their need to be with people sometimes overshadows their work. At times they meet with people just to be with them rather than with a view to getting the job done. Pleasing people is the first order of business, not spending time on tasks.

Type 4   Tom Cat

Tom Cats like to be left alone and set their own timeframes for getting jobs finished. They are independent and have little awareness of time or other people. They may find that others set time limits for them. Their use of time will reflect their low awareness of tasks and other people.

Answer the following questions:

- What do I know (or not know) about the people I work with?
- What do I know (or not know) about those I relate to regularly: clients, suppliers?

- What do these people know about me?
- What do I value and appreciate about these people?
- When did I last say that I valued them?

Depending on your answers, you may be able to discern whether you are more task oriented or people oriented. Are you a Road Runner or a New Pup?

Kickstart tip

Communicating clearly is important. Without it, when we are not with them people may delay action or, worse, do the wrong thing.

Most people assume that communicating is simple and straightforward. In fact, it's extremely difficult. Poor communication can lead to inadequate, inaccurate, delayed or non-existent information. To be successful, clear communication is vital. It's an essential part of your time management strategy.

> How well we communicate is determined not by how well we say things but how well they are received.
> Andrew S. Grove, Intel Corp.

Discussion with staff or clients is essential where it involves new work, and the timetable is an important factor. You need to be certain that your schedule will allow you to fulfil the client's needs, or to find alternative approaches. Additionally, you must ensure that the staff who will be involved in helping to produce the work understand the client's needs.

In any client-facing service it is always tempting to jump at the client's request. The client is, after all, 'king'. However, jumping without understanding is likely to cause an unnecessary crisis.

Jointly agreeing a realistic timetable and priority list with the client can be very useful and establishes a partnership. After all, the client may not appreciate how much work their requirement involves. Keeping staff informed of amendments to the work schedule is vital.

This communication is equally important in the opposite direction. Maintain close contact with your superior when engaged on a new or difficult piece of work. Alert him or her to any difficulties immediately they arise so that the time schedule can be adhered to, or adapted slightly if necessary.

Investing in consultation skills, for yourself or your staff, is a good plan. If you involve your team in communication skills training you can save hours of time. The cost is soon offset by improved dialogue and clearer understanding. Loquacious speakers should be encouraged to be brief (see Chapter 9 on meetings).

Kickstart tip

The most successful people employ the best people to work for them. Then they can go shopping!

Joking apart, this is very true. The greatest talent you can possess is the ability to spot talent in other people.

How to make your clients love you

Kickstart tip

Always welcome clients warmly. Some of them may be stressed about things they will not divulge immediately. By showing interest you accelerate the process by which they come to trust you.

When you meet someone for the first time and they give you a business card, write the date of the meeting on the back so that you can refer to it the next time you are writing to them. This may be as much as six months later. They will be so impressed that you remembered the date!

When in the office and able to do so, answering your own phone personalizes client contact. If you can't do it, divert the calls to your voicemail. This allows you to retrieve calls from wherever you are and get the message first hand. This maximizes clear communication, and also avoids delayed and distorted messages.

Managing staff

Effective staff management has the short-term aim of getting jobs done correctly and on time. At a higher level there is the long-term aim of nurturing or growing juniors. This is sometimes overlooked, but is ultimately more important if the business is to endure and prosper.

Nurturing your staff is an inherent part of management, delegating and encouraging people to take more responsibility. You can use your time more profitably and efficiently to win new business, the more skills you pass on to younger colleagues.

The main points to remember when managing staff, or for staff managing bosses, are:

- Create a working relationship that permits optimum job performance.
- Clarity – establish a clear aim and know your objectives.
- Definition of role – job descriptions help specify and protect autonomy.
- Maintain a flow of information – to confirm that work is progressing smoothly or to raise potential problems promptly.
- Insist on consistency – particularly when dealing with people who tend to change their mind.
- Contribute to team building – it helps to have a common purpose.
- Show respect for others – focus on the person's traits, for example prepare written work for those who are 'readers'; for 'listeners' spontaneous meetings are more likely to achieve your objective.

How to prompt self-sufficiency

Results are dependent on people. It is therefore important to use the right people and use them well. The key is to brief them properly. This may take you some time at first, but people will never be self-sufficient if they are not shown what to do. Instead of providing instant solutions, refuse to give easy answers. Throw things back at people asking, 'What do *you* think should be done?'

This usually prompts them to suggest alternatives. 'Well, I suppose this or that might suit. Which one of these works?'

Again, refuse to be drawn. Ask 'Which solution do *you* think is best?' If pressed, people often volunteer a perfectly acceptable way forward. Such an exchange may produce an immediate solution.

If this is your consistent response, people will change their approach and begin suggesting alternatives and eventually, when their confidence grows, they will work the answer out for themselves.

In many creative businesses, people fall naturally into three main groups. There are Finders, Minders and Grinders. The Finders are the leaders who go out and seek the business, make contacts, form alliances and bring back the projects. The Minders manage the shop, the teams and the work. The Grinders actually get on with the job of delivery.

A successful company, or even a household, cannot survive without a mix of all three. But do you have Grinders doing the work of the Minders, or vice versa? Are the Finders really Minders in disguise? Pay attention to people's natural gifts and use them wisely. Where appropriate, provide skills training so that people work willingly and successfully.

Avoid situations where people have to force themselves to do things. This makes for a hugely stressful atmosphere and large amounts of time being used unproductively. The smooth running of any establishment depends on positive interaction between colleagues. If they do not mesh, there will be difficulties.

Monitoring staff

There are times when throwing a problem back at staff will not work. In some cases you need to take a few minutes, or longer, to explain something. Setting people on the right track is always worthwhile. Although it takes time, it is a classic case of wise investment now yielding much more in the future.

The side effect of empowerment or self-sufficiency is that mistakes will be made and some actions taken that may not be appropriate. It is vital that you do not blame or belittle people's efforts. This is a sure-fire way of making them avoid risk taking in future. Discuss calmly with them how the decision was arrived at and what lessons can be learned.

You should be aware of and sensitive to inter-office rivalries. Don't encourage favouritism. Particular attention should be paid to the risk of showing partiality to those team members with whom you find it easiest to get on. This causes resentment and loss of productivity.

If some team members are dragging their feet, not following procedures, or demotivating others, disciplinary procedures should be instigated swiftly. If you have genuine misgivings about someone's behaviour, act without delay to avoid the further spread of negativity.

Having a clear policy as to team structure, roles and responsibilities avoids time being wasted in confusion or politics. It also provides clear paths of action for future occasions.

Motivating staff

Reward excellence by providing incentives and awards when measurable objectives are exceeded. This encourages a growth mentality among staff and team members and allows them to share in your prosperity. It also leaves you with less motivational work to do.

Building a culture of appreciation and reward, to minimize the loss of valued staff, helps to keep morale high. It saves time and money that would otherwise be needed to replace and retrain those who leave.

Ask for ideas from other people in the company and use them. Make sure that the idea creator gets the kudos for it! Remember to give recognition: 'Well done!' Even if you initiated the process, boost staff confidence and competence. It is essential that people take satisfaction from the whole process.

Minding staff

You look after your staff so they will look after you. You want to work effectively and that requires support from your staff. Perhaps you have experienced employees who think that putting work above all else makes them superior to others who do not. In fact, in the context of time management the reverse is true.

Colleagues and staff who are always at work may have stress in their lives from damaged relationships or health issues. They believe in working long days and longer nights because they 'love' their work. Their primary motivation actually has less to do with the project and more to do with the praise and recognition they receive. They seek approval and they want to be needed.

Wanting to feel valued and appreciated at work is fine, but if you rely on work for a sense of self-worth you are exposing yourself to risk. You are at the mercy of the whims of your superiors. You may desire praise from colleagues and senior staff, but if you do not always receive it you become demotivated.

Introducing boundaries

When your closest friends are your colleagues, you are in danger of your entire support network being in the office. That may be inevitable since you spend so much time there. Relationships in the workplace, and friendships, like office romances, should be treated with care. These can easily sour when vying with others for attention, raises and promotions.

Until the twentieth century, work was secondary to other parts of life. Even the Puritans considered work as a means to an end – the end being God. With the collapse of traditional cultural structures like family and religion, a vacuum has been created that work has grown to fill. Job satisfaction studies over the past two decades indicate that people are looking for identity, purpose and meaning in their work. Only a few find those things.

If you allow yourself, or your staff, to work for goals that are only found in the workplace – to improve your reputation or to make more money – you will not retain a good balance and all you will have is endless work. It is therefore vital to draw a distinct boundary between your life at work and your life outside.

Decisions, decisions

Decisions are a key time waster. The golden rule, when managing staff or in any leadership situation, is that the leader must be able to *take* decisions and not *make* them. The root of the word 'decision' means to cut. Once a decision has been *taken*, it must be *made* to work. Better the manager who takes a decision, even if it is a risky or difficult one, than the one who takes no decision at all.

The most effective leaders get only one out of three decisions right! But the reason they are successful is because they make even the poor decisions into good ones by working on them. The key is action, to take the decision, and then not to waste time worrying about whether it was a bad one. Staff are more motivated when they have a strategy to follow. Slow decision taking is a great stressor because indecision saps the morale of the team.

How to spot the high maintenance people in your life

Things, inanimate objects, can be dealt with efficiently, but this doesn't apply to people. You may be able to decide what to do with a piece of paper in ten minutes; people sometimes need much more time. People have to be dealt with *effectively*.

Of course you value your children, partner and friends highly; you rate them as 'important'. This means that when they have a problem you will treat it as a 'priority'. Whenever possible, you will stop what you're doing and give them the time and attention they need. If you're in the middle of a project at work, you promise yourself that you'll make up the time in the evening or at the weekend. But what if the problem can't be solved easily? Some urgent situations lend themselves to a 'quick fix', but in the case of illness, divorce or bereavement, a much larger commitment over a long period of time may be required.

In these cases, much though you love those concerned, you may have to develop additional skills in dealing with the High-Maintenance People (HMPs) in your life.

Typical HMP behaviour is where a one-off gesture is made. However small or simple, an HMP takes it as an on going commitment that the act will be repeated for the foreseeable future.

When encountering the situation for the first time most people are taken by surprise. The typical HMP believes that if you have offered to bring them a coffee one morning, you will be prepared to do so every morning for the rest of your life! They assume that you are delighted to be of service and have no appreciation of the fact that you have many other more important demands on your time.

In relation to time management, you need HMPs like Eskimos need fridges. HMPs come in various guises: family, friends, colleagues, clients and staff. The most difficult to deal with are client HMPs. Everyone needs clients, but at what stage do clients cease to be profitable and start to cost you money?

The best way of assessing HMPs is by scrupulous time recording. Keeping a time sheet for yourself makes you record every single hour of the day on the sheet to see what you've done. This helps identify high maintenance clients. For instance, if you've agreed to bill a job for 20 hours but it actually takes 30 hours to do the work, effectively you have done 10 unchargeable hours' work. It doesn't take a mathematician to work out that you won't be in business for long, or hold down your job, if you allow this situation to prevail.

Assertive techniques

The techniques you use for dealing with interruptions can be effective here too. HMPs tend to be bullies and despise the weak.

Want to avoid getting caught by an HMP in person or on the phone? Create a boundary. Explaining that you have a meeting starting in a few minutes should help. Offer to see if anyone else can deal with the request.

Buy yourself some time. If an HMP asks, 'Are you able to work this weekend?', answering 'I have plans' is sometimes easier than a straight 'No'. Never say 'Yes' to an HMP unless you really are prepared to give up your freedom.

Don't forget the power of silence. It leaves space for both parties to experience what is said and what is happening between them.

Avoid rambling. Instead, state simply what you think or what you want. Be specific and after making the point, stop. Keep reminding yourself of the purpose of the communication.

Drawing on my fine command of language, I said nothing.
Robert Benchley

Awkward situations

When dealing with awkward situations, behaviour is a strong influence. Imagine for a moment that a member of staff makes a suggestion about a way to tackle something. If your first response is, 'Oh come on, what a ridiculous idea. That has no chance of working at all!', the person will either back down or retaliate aggressively and you'll be facing each other with bayonets fixed.

If your response is something like, 'Well, that idea has its merits, but I'm not sure it's going to get us the result we need', although you are still disagreeing, the employee will probably accept your comments and the discussion can continue rationally.

The content and meaning of both responses are the same – you don't buy it! But the behaviour – the way it is delivered – is entirely different. And it is the behaviour that evokes the response. The most sensible reply to either of these is along the lines of 'OK then, it was just a suggestion. What do you propose?'

Kickstart tip

To help diffuse a potential conflict situation, listen non-emotionally to the content rather than react to the behaviour. Focus the discussion on the content.

Difficult clients, dissatisfied staff

Weed out difficult clients by giving awkward ones the choice of staying or leaving. Don't run the risk of wasting time with a dissatisfied customer. Consider ending any relationship that is consistently keeping you awake, dragging you down or draining you. Seek professional help and advice earlier rather than later. Whatever you do, deal with it.

Allow staff who want to leave to do so promptly and without regret. If a support team is to be really supportive, all members must be fully committed. Those who are not will leave eventually anyway. For more on this and related subjects, see *Kickstart Your Corporate Survival* in this series.

Summary

The keys to successful people management:

- Always think about the people aspects of everything.
- Keep a list of possible motivational actions in mind.
- See the process of communicating as continuous and cumulative.
- Do not be censorious about what motivates others.
- Beware of HMPs and easy options – they can cost you dearly in time and money.
- Watch the way you react to people – consider the content and not the behaviour.
- Evaluate what works best for you and for your group/company.
- Ring the changes in terms of methods of managing people so as to maintain interest.

Chapter 8

How to be Time Efficient with Technology and Paperwork

Technology – the knack of so arranging the world that we need not experience it.

Max Frisch, 1911–91

Time management when applied to IT falls broadly into two categories: *operational techniques* and *organizational habits*. By operational techniques I mean time-saving tips (such as becoming familiar with available shortcuts) so that the operator is as effective as possible. Organizational habits relate to time invested in good housekeeping so that the computer works efficiently as a time-saving tool.

The last time somebody said, 'I find I can write much better with a word processor,' I replied, 'They used to say the same thing about drugs.'

Roy Blount, Jnr

Making best use of your time means making optimum use of the technology you have at your disposal. Current statistics show that while 99 per cent of workers are computer literate in terms of basic Windows and email functions, they make use of as little as 30 per cent of the IT capability at their disposal. Because people are so busy at work they need computers to take the strain, but then they have to find time to keep up with changes and learning new skills.

Working with IT requires confidence and everyone should aim to have a working knowledge of the latest software packages, time savers and short cuts. Most people have access to (but don't always take advantage of) training. Use any opportunities you have to exploit in-house training facilities and courses (or equivalent outsourced workshops arranged by your employers). They will be invaluable aids to making best use of your office systems.

To err is human, to really foul things up requires a computer.

Anon.

Operational techniques and time savers

To make effective use of IT you need to know what the software does. Seek training if necessary. Become familiar with IT features such as mail-merge and templates. Email – don't memo. Use address book, groups etc. Print copies only as needed.

Time taken to become familiar with shortcuts on the PC will save hours of 'click time'. These can usually be found via the 'Help' menu.

Some companies may have set up computers with an auto-fax program. If so, spend time becoming familiar with this time-saving device. It is useful because no paper is generated and only one machine is used for two functions.

Use a scanner to scan in signatures. These can be inserted into a fax or any other document that may need to be faxed, but is not advisable if you are going to send the document as an attachment to an email, since the signature could easily be removed by an unscrupulous person.

> It's easy to cry 'bug' when the truth is that you've got a complex system and sometimes it takes a while to get all the components to co-exist peacefully.
>
> Doug Vargas

Organizational tips

If you use computers correctly, you can save yourself huge amounts of frustration. Some simple time saving devices include:

- Keep the hard drive as empty as possible. The less it contains, the faster it works. You company's IT department should be able to assist with this and maybe a simple request will get them on your side and make them feel appreciated.
- Regularly review your software to see if you have the most up to date versions. Put in a request for these if not, but do make sure that the new version will be compatible with existing software.
- Always back up the most vital files and data on to a CD rewriter or zip drive. This should then be stored on an external archive device (i.e. another computer or a second rewritable CD). Ideally these should be kept in a secure place. Most large companies will have their own back-up system – but if not, save sensitive files on to a floppy disk or other external media.

- Unless absolutely necessary, run only one program at a time. By keeping the task bar at the bottom of the screen as clear as possible, you'll find that the computer will work faster.
- By removing on to disk the majority of extraneous fonts you will save time wondering whether a document will look better in a different font. Most documents are produced in the top five universally used fonts. They are universally used because they are easy to read and not 'arty'. (Of course, if you work in graphic design this tip is not appropriate!)

Emails and time-saving tips

Since emails currently threaten to obliterate all other forms of communication, it is vital to stay on top of them. This means dealing with them ruthlessly. (See Chapters 3, 4 and 6.)

Clear the 'in' box every day. Allocate items that are time critical and then the pending items that will require work later. Delete any that are not relevant or important.

Unsubscribe from email lists. If you become an expert unsubscriber, you automatically become an expert at clearing the clutter in your inbox!

Another fabulous tip is to copy (cc:) or blind copy (bcc:) a message to yourself when responding to emails arranging a meeting or promising a response. This gentle reminder of a commitment previously made is invaluable. It saves time and possible embarrassment in case an arrangement slips.

Kickstart tip

Ration yourself to reading your emails two or three times a day – early morning, midday and late afternoon. This way reading messages as soon as they flash on the screen is avoided and your concentration on the task in hand is not interrupted.

The email system you use and how reliable it is may not be within your control. But whatever it is, check that you have the latest version, so full use can be made of all the sections. These are generally found under menu headings such as 'Message' or 'Tools'. These include various time-saving features, such as:

- Create a filing system for emails received from regular correspondents. Depending on your email system, this can either be done within the email program itself or by creating a new file or folder in Windows.
- Blocking unwanted messages. By setting up barriers supplied with your email package, specific email addresses will be blocked. Beware of opening messages from unidentifiable sources, particularly with attachments. These can contain viruses or micro-programs that can access and send to a third party information from your computer.
- Continually delete messages that you've already dealt with and empty the deleted items folder regularly.
- Keep the 'dealing' and 'dumping' rule firmly in mind (see later in this chapter), otherwise you'll struggle to find what you actually want in the squelchy swamp that remains.

- Compress files if they are going to be sent as email attachments. This will reduce the upload time while transmitting this information, and the download time for you if someone sends you a large file that has already been zipped. Zip and Stuffit are well-known programs and Microsoft Windows includes a compression tool in its latest version.

Kickstart tip

When sending people compressed files as email attachments, advise your recipients in the body of the email with which device the file has been compressed. This saves a phone call later on asking whether you used 'Squash it', 'Zap it' or 'Crush it'!

Mobile technology

Mobile technology can save you masses of time if used wisely. Times and locations of meetings can be changed at the last minute, for example, even while you are travelling to a meeting.

Diary software is becoming increasingly sophisticated. These packages allow for co-ordinated meetings with other colleagues and the ability to match available times. Making optimum use of your own and others' time is an example of the sophistication of time management techniques coupled with advanced technology.

DIY

A related matter is the fact that now few people have access to secretarial support. If it is available, that support is often limited. Research shows that in most large firms fewer than 20 per cent of managers have personal assistants. Many PAs have responsibility for looking after a number of managers or even an entire department.

The result is that today you are most likely to be responsible for your own admin. You are probably expected to look after your own travel bookings and other similar arrangements. This can create a squeeze on your time and is probably not the most efficient use of it.

Has technology gone too far?

K I S S – Keep It Simple, Stupid.

Technology is advancing so fast that recent research shows that only about 30 per cent of the IT capability you have is actually used. If you were capable of using 90 per cent of your existing technology maybe more working time would be saved – but how long would it take to reach such a level and would this be appropriate or viable?

Some companies have introduced so many IT-based activities that staff are able to do almost everything from their desks. By expeditious use of IT you certainly should improve your productivity and the management of your time.

However, at a seminar I attended not long ago, the speaker was having misgivings about the fast-changing effects that technology is having on our lives. He commented, 'With progress moving so fast, I expect we will soon find commodes fitted to our workstations and robots circulating our offices with food and drink trolleys. We will not be required to leave our desks at all. Ultimately, of course, we will lose the use of our legs, if not our bowels. Is this really good time management?'

Coping with paper

> I like [paper] work: it fascinates me. I can sit and look at it for hours. I love to keep it by me: the idea of getting rid of it nearly breaks my heart.
>
> Jerome K. Jerome, *Three Men in a Boat*, 1889

According to Jeffrey Maher, the author of *Time Management for Dummies*, we can dispose of 60 per cent of our desktop papers and 80 per cent of the desk drawer contents. This is an impressive statement.

Kickstart tip

In order to control your paperwork, you need to ask yourself four key questions:
- What information is important?
- What form does it need to be kept in?
- How long does it need to be kept?
- Who needs to have access to it?

To keep control of paper, you need self-discipline and organization. You may at times have felt that you were about to collapse under the weight of piles of paper on your desk. There is nothing more dispiriting than this. Being faced with stacks of paperwork on entering the office is enough to depress the most conscientious worker.

The best and swiftest method of tackling the problem of paper (before it becomes a crisis) is to use the 4D approach. This is really as simple as it sounds.

- Deal with it (it's probably urgent and overdue anyway).
- Determine it (a future action – don't return it to the pile).
- Deposit it (file it).
- Discard it (dump it in the bin – if it isn't valuable today, it won't be valuable tomorrow).

Deal with it

This is where you use the once-only rule. Pick up a piece of paper and deal with it. *Now*! Not later, not tomorrow. What needs to be done? Remember decisions – take a decision and make it happen. Does the piece need your signature? Do you need to raise a cheque to send it off for processing? Does it need answering – if so, will a quick phone call suffice? Do you need to compose a letter? Whatever the answer – deal with it at once.

Kickstart tip

If you are likely to find this difficult, use a red pen and put a dot in the top right-hand corner of the page each time you pick up a piece of paper. This way, by the end of the week, you can see which pieces have 'measles'.

Determine it

Taking a decision about future action is smart time management (this is important when applied to people as well as paper). Determine where to direct it. There should be no more than a few possibilities. It might be that you forward it to someone. If it has potential value for reference you need to file it. It might be wholly unnecessary, in which case – dump it.

Deposit it

Use the filing cabinet! If the piece of paper is an article that you've been meaning to read for weeks, highlight the relevant section and file it under the appropriate heading or in the 'to be read' file. If you think it might have a use for future reference, file it in a retrievable place.

Discard it

When in doubt, throw it out. Use the dustbin! Don't accumulate unnecessary paper. By continually reviewing and processing information, things shouldn't pile up and clutter your mind or desk. Anything that is left over is probably of limited value, so you're not likely to need it (see clutter busting later in this chapter).

Kickstart tip

To avoid collecting piles of paper that we don't know how to deal with, take the decision whether or not to save it. File it or fling it.

A simple and available tip for anyone is to use the recycle bin. Asking yourself if the piece of text at your fingertips really has value forces you to think. Does it really need filing? Can it be disposed of.

Reading

Kickstart tip

Anything worth reading should fit on one side of an A4 sheet of paper.

The quickest way to take control of your reading pile is to keep nothing for longer than two week's. If at the end of that time you haven't read it, ask yourself if it is still important. If it really isn't relevant, pass it on or throw it away.

Limit the size of the reading pile in the first place. A good tip is to date the relevant article, magazine or piece of paper – twice! Record the date when you received it and the date by which you need to have read it (if it is time critical). That way you avoid losing it or mislaying it if you have a deadline. If it is left on your desk, it may get forgotten or hidden.

> There was a time when the reader of an unexciting newspaper would remark, 'How dull is the world today!' Nowadays he says, 'What a dull newspaper.'
>
> Daniel J Boorstin, *Time Image*, 1962

Filing

Filing papers is something everyone dislikes. It is one of the C list tasks that you may find you can't get around to. You have to employ all the time management devices available to get yourself to do it – chunking, treats, the ten-minute rule, the hated task. Using a simple but effective system can help reduce those piles of paper (see Chapter 9 on knowledge management).

> It's true hard work never killed anybody, but I figure why take the chance?
>
> Ronald Reagan, interview, 1987

Clutter busting

Kickstart tip

In-tray actions
- Stop or divert unwanted items.
- Dispense with the in-tray altogether, since it encourages others to pass on work to you.

- Introduce the 'once-only' rule – deal with each piece of paper only once.
- Batch where possible (another version of blocking or chunking) – put all papers together that relate to one subject (accounts, sales, staffing etc.).

A clean desk does not signify an empty mind! Most people function more efficiently and effectively at a clean, well-organized workstation. Huge piles of papers do not mean that you are an industrious individual. You will continually be sidetracked by all the different files and bits and pieces. This actually prevents you from working on what's really important.

Kickstart tip

Clear the desk and keep it that way: only the most often used items should be accessible. If the desk is clear when starting a task, apart from the papers you are working on, you are less likely to get distracted and feel stressed.

Ban clutter! Is there clutter on your desk, in your home, in your life? If so, make time to clear it. It is amazing how virtuous you will feel. If you are unsure, start with a small step – turn out a filing cabinet or a desk drawer and see the difference. Watch the space grow and enjoy the feeling of satisfaction that comes with it.

Clearing the clutter from your live is liberating. This doesn't apply just to your computers, desks or offices – it is just as valid with clothes. Clutter takes up space on your desk and in your head.

Dealing with junk mail should be mentioned here. A huge amount of time can be lost because you are distracted by the latest offer from a mailshot that has landed on your desk. Time equals money and junk mail is another time bandit! If you have a serious addiction to junk mail, perhaps you should consider registering with the Mailing Preference Service (tel: 020 7766 4410 or www.mpsonline.org.uk) to get your name off the direct marketing lists.

Setting boundaries, again

If you make a conscious effort to limit the flow of information, you will be taking proactive steps towards controlling paperwork. Try not to receive or file more information than is necessary.

Setting yourself an assigned time to do an annual review of paperwork is one way of tackling the problem of overload. Have you any idea of what you are hoarding? Is there a lot of outdated material that can be thrown out? The risk likely to be incurred by throwing things out is much less than the potential risk of stress from information overload.

Try not to burden others with unnecessary information. If you are neat and concise with the information you distribute, people will pay more attention to you.

Kickstart tip

Don't allow paper to encroach on a day off by opening a briefcase. Nor should you switch on the computer, check your mail or read the diary. If you want to be an effective time manager, the object of time off is to get away from work totally.

Before attempting to enjoy your free time, remove all traces of work. Put your briefcase away, move the papers to another room or place them in a drawer. No one needs to be reminded of the work that has to be done.

Review any newspapers and magazines that you've accumulated. Are you really going to read them? Do they inspire, relax or excite you? If you've collected any depressing material, dump it right away.

Summary

Technology

- Become familiar with your computer and use time-saving tips and devices.
- Control emails – don't let them control you.
- Faxes – use them efficiently.
- Mobiles – take full advantage of the 'anywhere' office.
- K I S S – keep it simple.

Paper

- The 4D approach: Deal with it; Determine it; Deposit it; Discard it.
- Reading matter – only keep papers for two weeks.
- Filing – use a simple system and keep it up to date.
- Clutter busting – the benefits of clearing out and creating space.
- Set boundaries – this helps you maintain your time management skills.

Chapter 9

Meetings and Knowledge Management

> Meetings are indispensable if we don't want to do anything.
>
> J. K. Galbraith

Most people attend more meetings than they would wish to. No organization exists that does not have meetings, conferences, committees, working parties and seminars. Out of the workplace most of us get involved at some time or other in activities that involve attending meetings – neighbourhood watch, charities, church groups, children's school activities etc. The greater the number of organizations you are involved with, the more likely it is that you find yourself co-opted on to committees and expected to attend meetings.

To minimize the amount of time used when attending meetings, the best solution is to make them work for you. Meetings are not everyone's favourite activity. Wouldn't we all like to have a fiver for every tedious meeting we've attended over the years? Meetings can be hard work, boring and end up serving no purpose whatsoever.

> When I die, I hope it's in a meeting. The transition from life to death will be barely perceptible.
>
> Anon.

Managing meetings

A colleague and I meet regularly at an advisory board meeting held in London. We had been complaining loudly about the number of meetings we each attended in the course of the average year and had agreed that the majority were largely a waste of time.

'It's all down to the chair in most cases,' my colleague remarked glumly, as we settled in our places. 'A meeting properly organized and run can work so well. It's an effective device for saving time and progressing goals.'

This is absolutely true, but only where there has been careful planning beforehand. As effective time managers, we discussed the issue further and made the following observations.

Meetings vary enormously, from where they are held, the numbers attending, the formality of the setting, to the content of the agenda and follow-up procedures. Many of us hate attending meetings but have yet to find an alternative way of taking decisions. If you are invited to a large number of meetings you get the feeling that you are of some importance.

It is ironic that for all the complaints voiced on this subject, the moment you learn that a meeting is being held to which you are not invited, instead of sighing with relief, you feel anxious and insecure!

Some deadly meeting sins:

- **Time leaks** – the meeting may not start on time, or it might run way over its appointed end. What really counts is what is achieved between those two time poles.

- **Unfocused agenda** – this is the meeting from hell, it goes nowhere. It has no agenda and has wide-open items for discussion such as 'old business' 'new business' and 'any other business'.
- **Idea assassins** – meetings where participants are quick to criticize an idea before they've had a chance to hear it through and give it consideration. In this situation, some good ideas never make it to the crawling stage, let alone the running.

Vladimir: That passed the time.
Estragon: It would have passed in any case.
Vladimir: Yes, but not so rapidly.
                              Samuel Beckett, *Waiting for Godot*, 1955

At best, meetings are simply a device for communicating and are held for a number of reasons: to inform, to elicit information from those present, to discuss and exchange views, to instigate change in knowledge, skills or attitudes, to air grievances and settle disputes, to progress tasks, to persuade or to act as a stimulus for creative thought.

Why do meetings fail? They fail if they are unnecessary, or are not sufficiently planned, the venue is inappropriate, the wrong people are present, the chairperson is ineffective, or the objectives of the meeting are unclear.

What can you do to improve the effectiveness of meetings so far as your time management skills are concerned?

It is good to shut up sometimes.
                              Marcel Marceau

In order to prepare thoroughly for a meeting, you need to consider the following aspects.

Structure the agenda

This is very important. Prepare an agenda for distribution or a hidden agenda for the chairperson. Make available all supporting documentation. Meetings do not go well without the content being specified and the agenda being circulated well in advance.

Set time limits

Obviously there are some meetings that are productive and go over the allotted time. But on the whole meetings should have a set start and finish time. This way you can control the time in relation to the number of items to be dealt with. Focus on what needs to be discussed first. Select the start time carefully and precisely: not too late and not too long.

Why is this meeting necessary?

Before putting a single word to the meeting announcement, make sure that the issues involved warrant a get-together. Could they be handled by email or phone calls? Always set a clear objective so that you can answer the question 'Why is this meeting being held?'

Preparation

Read all the necessary papers and insist that others do so too. This will avoid you having to go through something that should have been studied beforehand and keeps the meeting on schedule.

People

Who should be present and what role does each person have? Not everyone warrants an invitation. Give adequate notice to the expected participants. People should not be permitted to ramble but should keep to the topic. Only one person speaks at a time. Avoid allowing eight people to get locked in a conversational scrum.

Venue

Meetings go much more smoothly if the people who attend are comfortable and there are no interruptions. Organize refreshments beforehand and divert telephones before the start. People should not be allowed to leave early or arrive late, halfway through proceedings.

Chairing

If you are going to lead, lead. Many of the elements of good meetings come down to the direction offered by the meeting facilitator. In general, try to use a light touch. You may be the most important person present, but that does not mean that you can do most of the talking. When chairing a meeting you should be conscious of the cost to the company of people's time.

The chairperson may find that the meeting fosters issues not originally on the agenda. If those come up, it's a good plan to place them in a 'parking lot'. That way if there's time at the end of the meeting and everyone wants to continue you can go on. If not, the items can be earmarked for the next gathering. Effective chairpersons keep loquacious speakers in check. At the end of the meeting the chairperson summarizes what the meeting has achieved and fixes the date for the next.

The results of effective meetings are positive and a good chairperson will ensure that everything occurs promptly, efficiently and properly. Minutes should be issued within 24 to 48 hours. Action points should be marked with completion dates and the initials of the person responsible in the action column. Prior to the next meeting a check should be made to ensure that the action points have been dealt with.

Jargon

Jargon is the enemy of good communication. While it is common to use jargon in most meetings, this is not always helpful and should be avoided. It is 'professional slang' and while creating useful shorthand for people within the group, it is dangerously misleading to those who do not understand the message.

People are often reluctant to demonstrate their ignorance by asking for an explanation. Speaking clearly and simply in words that everyone can understand is courteous and essential. When speaking at meetings, do not talk down from a superior position of expertise. This quickly alienates those present and promotes a negative attitude.

Where did the chairs go?

Some companies copy the Xerox method of meetings where all chairs are removed from the room. Meetings are conducted standing, starting and finishing according to a bell. This is regardless of how many people have turned up on time.

I have to confess that I hate the stand and deliver approach. I've tried it and while it does keep the meeting succinct, it can be uncomfortable and difficult to manage, particularly when having to juggle a bundle of paperwork. However, it is likely (if you have not already done so) that you will encounter a standing meeting at some stage in your work. For some it is a preferred option – why not try it and see if it works for you?

When working on a large and high-profile project, I remember that we held very quick, five-minute meetings every morning. These were simply for each of us on the committee to advise what we were going to do that day. This is a variation on the 'stand up' meeting. By declaring (going public on) our intentions to the team, it encouraged us to work to schedule and get things done. It also helped with motivation. This is more about personal effectiveness than time management relating to meetings, but it does have a relevance here.

Meetings where travel is involved

Meetings need to be controlled in terms of time when traveling is involved. Try to segment time – divide the diary into days when meetings can be fixed and other days when you remain at your desk. This is particularly important if you spend some of your time working in a different location from your main business address. It's far too easy to end up having several days at a time where you are spending hours in travel time for one/two-hour meetings and using up a whole day in the process. You then have even less time to do the thinking/writing work that results from the meeting.

Many people who travel extensively overseas for business are viewed with envy by friends and colleagues at home. They may portray an image of jet-setting elegance, sitting on balconies in exotic locations sipping cocktails while enjoying panoramic views. Apparently they find time to squeeze in the odd meeting between such pursuits. In reality, the business traveller shuttles like a headless chicken between bland hotels and even blander office buildings.

An associate of mine described her hectic travel schedule: 'Many of us have this guilt-based compulsion to maximize the trip by squeezing in as many networking opportunities as possible. Before long we can be an expert on Cairo traffic jams, yet having never seen the Pyramids. We can be on first-name terms with the receptionists at the Athens Intercontinental Business Centre, but have only glanced at the heap of rocks on the hill that is the Acropolis.'

Kickstart tip

When engaged on business travel, build in a buffer zone of time to reflect and be quiet. It enables you to focus, recharge your batteries and avoid under-performance.

Another colleague told me, 'I found the more I travelled the more tired and irritable I became and the less I appreciated the privilege of experiencing so many amazing places, cultures and people. Now I have a discipline. For every four-day trip, I take a half day for me. My objective? To play leisure tourist for a few hours and absorb myself in the local culture, heritage, whatever.

The benefits? A greater appreciation of how lucky I am, a more chilled-out me heading for the airport and, in many cases, the respect of clients and work colleagues pleased that I was actually interested in their city and culture.'

At the other end of the scale, an executive employed by a large American multinational in the UK told me that non-US-based personnel get called to meetings in the US, at very short notice. Despite having good-quality in-house videoconferencing facilities that are used, the bosses at head office still want to see their executives face to face.

Being summoned on a regular basis – leaving Heathrow on Monday morning, attending a meeting on Monday afternoon and flying back on Monday evening – is a punishing schedule, and makes for difficult Tuesdays! These executives do fly first class and are chauffeured everywhere, but is this really good time management?

There is plenty of evidence to support the claim that a well-managed travel schedule does improve performance. If a trip is intelligently planned, with particular attention paid to timezone differences, the traveller arrives in good time for his (or her) meeting. His paperwork is prepared and (depending on the length of the flight) he has probably worked while on board. He may have had the opportunity to sleep and emerges refreshed from the journey. If he is staying for a few days, appropriate accommodation will have been booked. Spending time paying attention to the traveller's comfort gives the best chance of a high standard of performance while doing business.

In these days of heightened security alerts, travelling without delays or upset cannot be guaranteed, but these are matters that in the majority of cases are out of your control. If a carefully planned itinerary has been made, you have the greatest chance of staying in control of the trip. This is certain to be to the company and the individual's advantage and in terms of time management it is good practice.

Kickstart tips

If travelling abroad for meetings, plan arrangements realistically, bearing in mind the availability of people being visited.

- Check that the sequence of meetings to be accomplished is logical and in order of importance.
- Allow for travel problems beyond your control as well as anticipated problems, such as rush-hours, availability of parking facilities, etc.
- Pay attention to your personal stamina following a lengthy journey and appreciate the possibility of impaired performance.

Virtual meetings

Even if you are committed to working with clients abroad, there are alternatives to flying halfway across the world for essential update meetings. Videoconferencing systems save thousands in air miles and time for a relatively small investment. Training is available on how to make videoconferencing look professional. Advance planning (as for traditional meetings) is helpful, so that people sit in the right place, don't talk over one another and stick to a focused agenda, to save wasting time.

A number of good phone conference systems are also available. Video and teleconferencing should be part of any company's communications strategy. Managers should be asking, do we travel to this meeting or conduct it remotely?

The challenge is like any aspect of time management – whether to change your habits. If you live in London, there is no sense spending three hours at the airport for a one-hour meeting in Brussels.

Depending on the frequency of the meetings, it is up to each company to decide its policy with regard to face-to-face meetings. In most cases it would be judged best to have a face-to-face meeting in the first instance. Nothing compares to a personal encounter. It allows people to get to know each other, builds relationships and facilitates trust.

Once the relationships have been established, should regular meetings be required, it might be a better use of time to establish videoconferencing for all concerned. But remember that however useful and time efficient they are, video links will never replace chatting to colleagues and clients over a drink!

Effective and productive meetings

> The time to stop talking is when the other person nods his head affirmatively but says nothing.
>
> Anon.

In order to be effective, meetings have to have goals. Too many meetings degenerate into talking shops (particularly if they are institutionalized, such as weekly team meetings).

If there isn't enough to fill a weekly team meeting, don't be afraid to make them less frequent.

Draw a line under discussions that aren't reaching a conclusion and arrange for the key parties to meet separately and return with an agreed approach.

Always nominate an individual to be in charge of a project. 'Ownership' breeds responsibility. If there is no one clearly responsible for a project, then there is a reduced penalty for delay as no one catches the flack for failure.

A corollary of this is the more general management point that if a project is subject to repeated delays, don't be afraid to kill it. The money and time lost are a sunk cost while you are going forward. These resources might be better employed elsewhere.

Don't spend half a day documenting minutes after a meeting, but do email all of the participants with agreed actions, who has to execute them and when they have to be done.

Eighty percent of success is showing up.

Woody Allen

Over 80 per cent of a meeting is managed before and after it takes place. Assuming that you have all attended at least one meeting in the last few weeks, answer the questions below to test whether it was effective:

- Was it necessary?
- Were the objectives clear?
- Were those objectives met?

- Was time used efficiently?
- Did timing and venue permit optimum attendance?
- Was the agenda issued in sufficiently good time to be useful?
- Did it have sufficient indication of what the topics were about?
- Was proper time, or too much time, given to the topics?
- Was the agenda run in the order intended?
- Did extraneous material get added?
- Did the most appropriate people attend?
- Was sufficient material provided in advance?
- Did everyone feel they got the opportunity to contribute adequately?
- Were opinions actively canvassed?
- Were clarifications sought and given?
- Were action points summarized and agreed by all?
- Did everyone go away satisfied with the process?
- Did everyone feel that any objections had been properly noted?
- Were minutes succinct and free of unnecessary detail?
- Were they issued within 24/48 hours?
- Were actions, due dates and responsibility for action clearly shown?
- Did the chair and organizer (if different) work very much as a team?

Controlling information and knowledge

> The test of a first-rate intelligence is the ability to hold two opposed ideas in mind at the same time and still retain the ability to function.
>
> F. Scott Fitzgerald

If you were born organized, that's great. If, however, you are messy, there's nothing wrong with that – you just need to learn how to clear up fast! Going paperless is not the goal. The real aim is to identify how to manage information. You may say, 'I can find everything, so who cares that my office is a mess?' The answer to that is, 'What if you're not there?'

When getting organized, don't start with the old stuff. Start with today's mail, it will be tomorrow's pile! Organization is not a mystery, it is simply finding a method that works for each of us.

Most people don't want to work in a mess, but either they don't know how to keep tidy, they don't have time or they don't pay attention to it. You need to ask yourself what information is important, what form it needs to be kept in, how long it needs to be kept and who needs to access it.

There are tips on dealing with paperwork in Chapter 8. Another simple but ruthless system is F A T – go through every piece of paper and **F**ile it, **A**ct on it or **T**oss it.

Disorganization is also caused by an inability to take decisions. If you postpone decisions, you create clutter, either in your mind or on your desk, and probably both.

As discussed before, by using delegation all administrative functions associated with such areas as finance, book-keeping, credit control, information management and compliance paper-work can be dealt with so that your time is freed up for other tasks.

What to keep and how to find it

Make sure that all incoming information is put in one place, and I mean *all*. Mail, messages, journals etc. all should be in your in-tray and nowhere else. Empty that tray every time you come back to your desk. This shows people that you receive and act on your messages. If you work in a department, there is often a system where everyone's in-tray is kept in a central location. In addition you need an out-tray for items that are ready to be despatched, passed on to others or filed.

Record keeping, contacts and databases

With any established or growing business, people sometimes forget to plan for recording customer or client notes, potential business contacts and other information. As the company grows you may find that you are losing control of information. You should ask yourself the following:

- Do I know who everyone is? What information do I need to keep on clients, contacts and potential work providers?
- How should I prioritize whom I contact and how often? How can I maintain accurate records of who is in my network, what skills they have and what I can offer them?

In larger companies entire departments are responsible for such matters, but in smaller businesses it falls to staff members to shoulder these responsibilities and encourage others in the knowledge management culture.

One simple way of tackling the issues is to devise a form for clients, contacts, referrers and work providers covering such questions as:

- Where they met, what they do.
- Type of business, skills they have.
- Names of key people in their organization.
- Outline of initial meeting and reasons for relationship.
- Target outcome for development.
- Preferred follow-up/contact procedure.

Once this information is recorded it should be stored in a file (if paper has been generated) or electronically in a database.

Then you action your contact strategy. This is your plan for when and how to contact clients, potential clients and possible work providers. It should contain the following:

- When to contact clients/work providers/networkers.
- What the target is for contacting them.
- How to do this – email, phone call, newsletter, face-to-face meeting.
- How many contacts to be made each month.
- Categorize the contact in terms of likelihood of obtaining work.
- Draft income projection based on this information.

By keeping up to date with the company's network and potential clients, you are paying serious attention to helping the organization grow its business. You are setting goals that increase the company's likelihood of success. In some organizations it is possible that there is an established reward system in operation for this kind of information, so it can pay dividends to be scrupulous about keeping up-to-date records for the company's knowledge management.

Simple systems that work

Designing systems for everything – answering the phone, registering client details, raising invoices etc. – saves hours of time. The system must be followed every time and should be able to function without you. With the right systems in place, you should be able to take holidays without the place collapsing in your absence.

Filing systems should be so easy that you do the filing promptly, thus avoiding a backlog of unfiled papers on your desk.

The turnaround file

This is an invaluable device and can be adapted to suit many purposes. Turnarounds can be weekly, monthly or yearly. They can be purchased (concertina-type files) or be home made, simple cardboard wallets attached together by means of holes punched with split rings attached to link them together. They work exactly as described – by turning around. Weekly turnarounds need five pockets; monthly turnarounds require four pockets, yearly turnarounds require twelve pockets.

Having decided that you need a 'follow-up' procedure to avoid piles of papers accumulating, the turnaround can be used to great effect.

The weekly turnaround pockets are labelled Monday to Friday. Depending on the status of the item, date it and place it in the appropriate pocket. If it is the agenda to a meeting taking place on Thursday, file it in 'Thursday'. The same application is used for papers that require retrieval on a weekly basis (e.g. fortnightly meetings) and again for monthly papers. For another example, the annual insurance premium is filed in the month preceding its renewal date.

Follow-ups

This is simply a method of recording when a piece of paper should be looked at again. Record the date somewhere on the paper, such as the top right-hand corner. File the paper in the turnaround, so that on the date agreed you can decide whether action needs to be taken or has already been sorted. A simple example is a copy of a letter inviting an associate to a lecture. Diarize the date for checking the response. Mark the paper with the appropriate date and wait for it to appear when dealing with the turnaround.

Drop files

This is a very simple but effective system that has been mentioned earlier. Find a filing drawer and some drop files. Label the first twelve January to December. Label the rest 1 to 31. You now have somewhere to file things for this month (the report you need to read; those tickets for a conference; a note of a question to ask at next week's meeting; a birthday card.

Anything for next month, or the rest of the year, goes in the January to December sections. Each day as you sit at your desk, you deal with the contents of the day's file. At the end of the month, open next month's file and distribute the contents between files 1–31.

This system can be extended by creating hanging files for projects or customers you regularly deal with that you want to keep to hand.

Treasure chest

A useful device for 'ideas' is designating a file, drawer or other container for reference material that will be useful at some future date. One entrepreneurial friend of mine has his 'treasure chest of opportunities' in a drawer in his desk. It is full of cuttings, articles, ideas and 'triggers' for possible business ventures, partnerships, 'pie in the sky' inventions – anything and everything that floats in front of him and he wants to keep hold of. Sometimes they stay there for years, others he uses more quickly. Whatever the timescale, he always has lots of ideas to play with, numerous schemes to explore and future projects that he can put into practice. He reckons that it will keep him occupied and (he hopes) rich for the rest of his life. It could be described as a way of capturing serendipity!

For the hoarders among us, caution should be exercised when using this system, however. It is not a dumping ground for any extraneous matter that can't otherwise find a suitable home. It is strictly for information and prompts that will be useful and relevant at some point in the future. Any sign of old bus tickets, junk mail, last year's Christmas cards and out-of-date library tickets joining this collection, and the 'treasure chest' has been abused!

The brain dump

This is simply a paper-less system for holding ideas. Creative thinkers may be brimming with thoughts but weak on organization. When random ideas come into your head, never waste them. Whether it is vaguely relevant or specific, make a note of it by opening a new file on your computer. Label it with a subject or topic so that you can refer to it easily at a later stage. The name should be something relevant and remind you of the matter you had in mind at the time. The file will contain all thoughts and suggestions relating to any subject about which you have random ideas.

These may come to you at odd moments, when you've seen something on TV, or heard a remark on the radio, or noticed a quotation, a headline, a report in the press, a suggestion from a colleague, or benefited from a chance meeting with a friend. Anything that needs to be filed away as a mental note can be stashed safely in this way. It is a simple and quick way of storing information – it takes up little room, leaves your mind free and doesn't require rainforests to be destroyed. These random ideas can be used as and when required for whatever is appropriate: presentations, speeches, proposals or reports. If you suffer from 'overload' it is a great relief not having to remember. And if you regularly write articles and books, it is a particularly easy and efficient way of collecting material!

Summary

Meetings

- Beware the deadly meeting sins – time leaks, unfocused agenda.
- Structure the occasion – time limits, purpose, venue.
- Chairing – keep control, avoid drifting.
- Meetings and travel – focus on time efficiency.
- Alternatives – virtual meetings, videoconferencing.

Knowledge management

- Controlling information and knowledge – use the F A T system.
- Keeping records – maintain a simple database.
- Other systems that work – turnaround, follow-ups, drop files, treasure chest, brain dump.

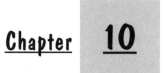

Keeping up the Good Work

> Regret for the things you did can be tempered by time; it is regret for the things you did not do that is inconsolable.
>
> Sydney J. Harris *Strictly Personal*

You probably started reading this book with the intention of learning some ways to achieve more and waste less time. To recap, let's go over some of the main points. Good time management is getting the optimum result in the minimum time.

Priorities

Never lose sight of priorities. If you can't set priorities you will approach everything with equal weight. Obviously some things *must* be more important than others and these are the items you need to handle first. You should choose your priorities by importance and urgency.

Set a ranking code (priority sequence) for all tasks:

A = Must do activities (essentials).
B = Beneficial, but not mandatory (important).
C = Unnecessary activities (optional).

Analyse the essential tasks and assign them a priority order, A1, A2, A3. Then do the same with the Bs and the Cs. Make sure those with whom you work understand, support (and if appropriate, agree) to your priorities. Review them and check them daily or weekly.

Time wasters

It is easy to allow time to slip by unnoticed. Identify and eliminate the time wasters. Have a look at the list of major time wasters and see which ones affect you:

- Can't say no.
- Crisis management: glitches, problems, catastrophes.
- Indecision, procrastination, poor communication.
- Inconsistent action, inefficiency.
- Interruptions, telephone, unnecessary meetings, visitors.
- Junk mail, unnecessary paperwork.
- Lack of information, objectives, management, delegation.
- Lack of priorities, procedure, systems, self-discipline.

Kickstart tips

How to pack for a holiday: put all the items you want to take with you on the floor, cut the number of items down by half, then pack. Result: a suitcase that will close easily!

How to get more done in a week: pretend there are only two and a half days available. List the jobs that have to be done. Delegate or dump the rest. Result: more time for important work.

Planning

You need to keep on top of things – you must have a plan! Remember your lists, schedule, diary. Always refer to your planner, log, to do list, – whatever system you use (Figure 10.1). If you always have your goals close at hand, you will be sure of what it is you have to do next.

Master the diary – find a way of keeping track of your time that suits you best, whether an electronic diary, monthly schedule or wall planner. Always allocate your most productive time of the day to top priorities. Don't allow others to erode that 'prime-time' slot.

To maintain your motivation level, keep a note of how you spend your time with a tracker sheet. Do at least one of these every week.

Watch how many lines you have in the average day; track how long you spend on each task on average. Keep an eye on the interruptions, how many and for how long. How many chunks of time were less than 15 minutes? How many times were you able to work for more than an hour without interruption? Are there any patterns you can see?

This will highlight how long tasks take, how frequently you have to allow for interruptions, how efficient you are at spending time on things that move you towards your goals and how much time you spend troubleshooting.

You should start with the most important task first. The only exception to this is that if the end results are equally valuable, do the easiest or shortest ones first. This is a way of building momentum. You can then concentrate better on the tougher tasks

Start	Length	What you did	Type
8.15	15	Deal with papers on desk, including searching for agenda for meeting with marketing dept.	Admin
8.30	10	Phone call to client regarding proposal	Sales
8.40	10	Look at emails and answer three, file seven for dealing with later	Admin
8.50	5	Interrupted by staff member arriving from head office	Admin
8.55	25	Fax received with proposed budget figures from accounts	Finance
9.20	15	First meeting with sales reps	Sales
9.35	25	Leave office for first meeting in town with new client	Admin
10.00	60	Meeting with new client	Sales

Figure 10. 1   Sample day log

because you will not have so many other tasks hanging over your head.

In the words of Jerome K. Jerome (*Thoughts of an Idle Fellow*, 1886), 'It is impossible to enjoy idling thoroughly unless one has plenty of work to do.'

Glitches, problems and crises

What can go wrong, will go wrong! The effective time manager always tries to anticipate potential problems where possible and act accordingly. Honesty helps: admit there is a crisis. There's no need to waste valuable time apportioning blame. Don't just react – think first.

Glitches are frequently mechanical, require logical thought and accurate information. Most glitches can be solved by pooling information and data, calling on experts to provide skills, knowledge and expertise. (Urgent tasks.)

Problems are deeper than glitches; they involve feelings rather than mechanics. In order to solve problems, you need to be objective, respect other people's feelings, suspend judgement and listen. Problems relate to policy, personnel and change. (Important tasks.)

Crises are the most serious, involving mechanical and emotional elements. They have deep implications for an organization, being both time sensitive and potentially damaging to the business and its workforce. If a crisis isn't fixed, people could face redundancy or the business might not be able to continue. The solution is rarely quick, but the intelligent manager takes firm decisions to limit damage while working out the best strategy for the future. (Urgent and important.)

When dealing with difficult/impossible things, think! Try using your brain as a problem box. Don't make the mistake of putting everything into the same box. Put one problem in a box by itself, so that when you lift the lid to look at it, there aren't lots more horrible things jumbled around inside about to leap out at you. If you learn to deal with one thing at a time, you will cope better and arrive at a workable solution more easily.

Delegating

Identify the task and the objectives. Decide on the person to do the task and ensure adequate resources and authority. Brief thoroughly and clearly (communication). Follow through by checking and feedback.

Decision making

Good teamwork is the ability to arrive swiftly at a consensus opinion. Begin by defining the problem. List possible solutions and their pros and cons. If you provide people with a common approach to decision making, the quality of decision making inevitably improves.

Organization

Without good personal organization it is difficult to manage your time effectively. Here are some of the most important elements to remember:

- Manage your environment – keep a tidy desk/office/mind.
- Handle less paper, handle it less often, cut down on junk reading.

- Communicate effectively on paper and in person – be clear and concise.
- Be conscious of time – keep a clock where everyone can see it.
- Make the daily 'to do' list flexible and the deadlines realistic.
- Be assertive, create a buffer zone, give yourself private time.
- Have simple and user-friendly office systems – avoid distracting clutter.

Maintenance and motivation

Kickstart tip

Realism is an important aid to time management.

Keeping motivated is sometimes a problem. You may have the desire to keep to your new resolutions and plans, but your willingness to focus and take action cannot be taken for granted. A positive state of mind requires constant effort and nurturing, including awareness of its vulnerability. Don't assume that once you have started to concentrate on your time management things will always go well and you'll never have another bad day.

You may suffer from the occasional bout of being overwhelmed. Don't panic – this will pass. If it's stress related, take some time out – get some rest or spend some time doing something inspirational. You may get bored; if so widen your horizons by planning some new strategy with different challenges. Lack of balance indicates loss of perspective. To avoid becoming disillusioned you need to focus on out-of-office activities. Withdrawal can be due to depression or feelings of being let down by others. The solution is to form a support team and approach others for help and advice.

Kickstart tips

- Don't assume that you will always be focused.
- If you have a problem, deal with it as quickly as possible.
- Identify whether it is technical, personal or policy related.
- Be flexible, adapt the system, adopt new techniques.
- Listen to others, ask for support, challenge ideas, facilitate change.

Now that you feel the benefits of good time management, don't slip back. These habits can be kept for ever.

Summary

Everything happens to everybody sooner or later, if there is time enough.

George Bernard Shaw

In conclusion, getting 'organized' is a great thing and a solution to perfect time management, provided that 'disorganization' is the problem in the first place. If the reason those hours disappear is due to boredom, worry, lack of motivation, stress or being overwhelmed, then you need to take other steps to help you. (See *Kickstart Your Motivation* in this series.)

Time management is personal and each of us interprets it in a different way. Depending on the type of person you are, you will identify time management in the way that makes sense to you. It cannot be applied generally. It is a positive thing and from this book I hope you've learned some methods of time control that will work for you.

With effective time management you should be able to gain some time. Energy, unlike time, is not fixed but physical and mental; the drive is variable. With good time control you can improve your energy levels. If you follow the guidelines in this book, energy can be conserved and better directed. In essence, you will have the ability to *create* time and achieve greater results. Don't waste it!

Index